More Praise for *The Art of Community*

"Powerful, practical, and inspiring. A modern articulation of, and advancement on, timeless wisdom. Emerging or veteran leaders who integrate these principles will build communities that are more resilient, passionate, and harmonious in the face of adversity and uncertainty."
  —**Alan Price, Founding Director, Global Leadership Initiative, Harvard Business School, and author of *Ready to Lead?***

"*The Art of Community* is a brilliantly intentional, well-composed plan for engaging and developing communities. This book is both an inspiration and a field guide for those who wish to connect deeply and build the communities our world so desperately needs. As I read *The Art*, I found myself drawn to possibilities that fed my soul. I see new ways to tie myself and my family to others in constructive and spiritually rewarding ways. *The Art of Community* promises to enrich our lives immensely through new insights into community, leadership, and personal growth."
  —**Thomas A. Kolditz, PhD, Brigadier General, US Army (ret.); Director, Doerr Institute for New Leaders; Founding Director, Leader Development Program, Yale School of Management; Founding Director, West Point Leadership Center; and author of *In Extremis Leadership***

"This book is full of rich wisdom and simple tools to help make community real. Our mission statement includes the word 'community,' but I never truly understood what it meant until reading this book. Too often we declare a community around affiliation without digging into the shared values and care for one another that make a real community."
  —**Jason Jay, PhD, Director, Sustainability Initiative, MIT Sloan School of Management, and author of *Beyond the Choir***

"A deeply thoughtful and compelling book that shares many insights with clarity, accessible examples, and ideas for implementation. I learned a lot."
  —**Lawrence Levy, former CFO, Pixar Animation Studios; cofounder, Juniper Foundation; and author of *To Pixar and Beyond***

"Charles Vogl's book is a lucid, ferociously intelligent, and readily accessible road map to building a more connected culture. Education about community and character has been subordinated in American education to myopic cognitive and commercial learning. The result everywhere around us is devastating, from unprecedented wealth disparities to rampant tribalism. This work points to a much-needed antidote."
—Marty Krasney, Executive Director, Dalai Lama Fellows

"A useful field guide to create durable and profound connections. It is an important undertaking, as isolation and loneliness are a root cause of the breakdowns all around us, including extreme violence."
—Peter Block, author of *Community* and *Flawless Consulting*

"I've personally experienced the magic that Charles Vogl creates in powerful communities. People feel genuine belonging and connection. Now he has written down the essential principles so that others may experience this magic themselves. I cannot imagine a more important subject for a book in a society where so many of us hunger for connection and community."
—Scott Sherman, Executive Director, Transformative Action Institute

"*The Art of Community* is an outstanding guide to creating and fostering the meaningful communities all of us need. As technology that allows us to physically detach from one another accelerates, it has become more important than ever to understand what community and belonging mean. Strong, mature communities benefit both individuals and humanity as a whole."
—Jonathan Knowles, Explorer in Residence, Autodesk, and host of the Autodesk IDEAS series

"If you are tasked with bringing families, neighborhoods, or organizations together, read this book first. In *The Art of Community*, author Charles Vogl reinvigorates a vision of community and the importance of social bonds to our well-being. In place of our convenient and transient associations, Vogl tells us how to establish relationships that are more meaningful and enduring."
—Michael O'Malley, author or coauthor of *Every Leader Is an Artist*, *The Wisdom of Bees*, and *Leading with Kindness*

The
Art of Community

The
Art of Community

*Seven Principles
for Belonging*

CHARLES H. VOGL

Berrett–Koehler Publishers, Inc.
a BK Currents book

Berrett-Koehler Publishers, Inc.
1333 Broadway, Suite 1000
Oakland, CA 94612-1921
Tel: (510) 817-2277   Fax: (510) 817-2278   www.bkconnection.com

Ordering Information
Quantity sales. Special discounts are available on quantity purchases by corporations, associations, and others. For details, contact the "Special Sales Department" at the Berrett-Koehler address above.
Individual sales. Berrett-Koehler publications are available through most bookstores. They can also be ordered directly from Berrett-Koehler: Tel: (800) 929-2929; Fax: (802) 864-7626; www.bkconnection.com
Orders for college textbook/course adoption use. Please contact Berrett-Koehler: Tel: (800) 929-2929; Fax: (802) 864-7626.

Distributed to the US trade and internationally by Penguin Random House Publisher Services.

Berrett-Koehler and the BK logo are registered trademarks of Berrett-Koehler Publishers, Inc.

Printed in the United States of America

Berrett-Koehler books are printed on long-lasting acid-free paper. When it is available, we choose paper that has been manufactured by environmentally responsible processes. These may include using trees grown in sustainable forests, incorporating recycled paper, minimizing chlorine in bleaching, or recycling the energy produced at the paper mill.

ISBN 978-1-62656-8419

Library of Congress Cataloging-in-Publication Data
Names: Vogl, Charles, 1974– author.
Title: The art of community : seven principles for belonging / by Charles Vogl.
Description: Oakland : Berrett-Koehler Publishers, [2016] | Includes bibliographical references and index.
Identifiers: LCCN 2016018838 | ISBN 9781626568419 (pbk. : alk. paper)
Subjects: LCSH: Communities. | Community organization. | Organizational sociology.
Classification: LCC HM756 .V64 2016 | DDC 307—dc23
LC record available at https://lccn.loc.gov/2016018838

First Edition
23 22 21 20 19 18   10 9 8 7 6 5 4 3

Project management, design, and composition by Steven Hiatt, Hiatt & Dragon, San Francisco
Copyeditor: Paula Dragosh   Proofreader: Tom Hassett   Indexer: Theresa Duran   Cover designer: DogEared Design

To Mr. and Mrs. Mwango, Mr. Puta, Mr. Davies,
and Luposhi village in Luapula Province, Zambia

Even before I knew it
you welcomed me when I was a stranger in a strange land
far from home and crying in the night.
May I offer to others what you gave to me
when you changed my life.

Contents

Draw the circle wide.
Draw it wider still.
Let this be our song.
No one stands alone.

Mark Miller and Gordon Light
"Draw the Circle Wide"

Preface

In my professional life, I work with leaders in tech, finance, government, and social change organizations to create meaningful change. Drawing partly from spiritual traditions, I help these leaders understand how they can build loyalty, strengthen identity, and live out shared values. When leaders create a robust and committed community, they build relationships that are effective and resilient. These relationships in turn can lead to profound change. This book is an extension of that work. It's primarily (but not exclusively) intended for those brave people who seek to bring others together to create something enriching, satisfying, and meaningful. Sometimes that something is a community that can shift the future of our planet. But let's put that aside for the moment.

It's only because I felt like an outsider for so long that I was able to write this book about community building and belonging. When I say, "outsider," I mean someone who wonders "will I ever have the friends I want" and "is there anywhere I'll ever fit in." I've felt so lonely that I've cried alone at night. In my early twenties, I accompanied my cousin Erin to her large, young, and hip church in Los Angeles because I was searching for a spiritual community. The service began with a downbeat from the contemporary praise band. In that moment, seemingly everyone, well over a thousand people in the auditorium, stood and raised their hands in the air and began swaying with the music. Halfway through that service, I no longer wanted to pretend that I was comfortable. I preferred something far more contemplative. Quietly, I sat down.

I still remember the looks and frowns directed at me sitting alone. It was clear that I didn't belong. Over the years, I have sought out many groups, looking for the right one, the one to which I would belong.

When I was twenty-five, I served in the US Peace Corps in northern Zambia, near the Congo–Zaire border. When I left home, I looked forward to meeting people as brave and adventurous as I wanted to be. The villagers welcomed me generously, but I felt lonely many nights, in a strange place with a different language and different food. Not fitting in, in that environment, was not a surprise. But I also remember the nights I sat around fire pits with other volunteers. Often there were tall stacks of beer crates nearby. In the background, a never-ending series of drinking games went on. One night, a Peace Corps volunteer I'll call Ralph turned to me and said, "I don't trust people who don't get drunk." Because I didn't drink alcohol, well, he didn't trust me.

From that conversation and several similar evenings, I understood that I didn't really fit in among those volunteers either.

After the Peace Corps I moved to New York City, still hoping to find the group to which I would belong. A pastor on Manhattan's East Side introduced me to wisdom from C. S. Lewis's lecture "The Inner Ring."[1] Lewis wrote that we all want to enter inner rings of exclusivity. These are groups that are more exclusive and cooler than the groups to which we already belong. The problem lies not in the rings themselves but in our desire and longing to get inside them. This desire drives good people to do very bad things. It's the unrecognized cause of a lot of unhappiness. Lewis further explains that, unfortunately, when we do get inside these exclusive rings, we always discover that there's an even more attractive and exclusive ring beyond. This pattern will continue forever unless we break it. This is the trap of the inner ring.

Lewis's solution was to find something we like to do and do it often. Then invite others to join us if they like doing that thing too. The people who join us will create a special type of relationship that allows us to escape the trap of the inner ring. That relationship is called friendship. I was inspired by the notion that if I could not find the right community, perhaps I could create it. At the time, I was producing, without sufficient skill or resources, what became an independent PBS documentary. I also organized other restaurant workers abused by a company that ignored labor laws. I came to understand that building community was important for success in both endeavors.

In my thirties, I went to graduate school at Yale to study religion, ethics, and philosophy. There I learned many ideas that had brought together people across the globe over millennia. I learned how Jews coalesced within a hostile empire, how Anabaptists stood up to the Roman Church at horrific cost, how Zen monastics still dissuade outsiders from joining their long-kept private rituals, how Jains maintain their radical compassion in a violent world, and how Green Nuns band together to celebrate a new theology for our relationship to earth. So many people over so many years have held together in brutal and murderous times. Often they were so successful that you can still meet their descendants today. It was inspiring to see how strong even small bands could remain, even while facing existential threat. There was so much to learn from them, lessons that applied just as easily to secular communities as to spiritual ones.

One thing that surprised me, when I arrived at Yale, was the discovery that its history and brand loomed so large that many other students, just like me, thought that they could never be good enough to truly belong there. We feared that, at any moment, someone would ask us to leave after revealing us to be the frauds we felt certain we were. There was a lot of loneliness and fear at Yale. With Lewis's wisdom in mind, my now wife Socheata and I chose to host dinners in our home every Friday night. We would cook a large multicourse dinner and serve it to anyone who would come.

That first semester there were many times when I was sure that we had made a silly commitment. Guests would cancel at the last minute. I would cook a feast and only three people would show up. I had to turn down invitations to all the other fun stuff on Fridays on campus and in New York. Over time, things changed. With perseverance and a lot of work, the dinners became popular. But after hosting well over five hundred people in our home, we were exhausted. Rather than give up the dinners, we built a team of volunteers to plan the menus, cook the meals, and set the space. Arjan volunteered to manage the appointed dinner leaders, and Sam would go on to manage the sponsors and guest lists.

While cooking dinners, sharing those meals, and cleaning our kitchen, I formed many of my dearest friendships. Those friends have traveled with me across countries and stood with me at my wedding. On my worst days, I call them so I don't cry alone. Sometimes, they cry in my living room. We are now to one another what my friend Nick calls "3 a.m. friends." We know that when we call each other at 3 a.m., we'll ask how we can help and then take action. We make one another so much stronger.

In my sixth year in New Haven, my friend Melo took me to lunch at the Yale Commons. Just the two of us sat at a long table on the north side, and he shared a special story with me. He told me that his first year at Yale had been the hardest of his life. He had come from the Philippines, and the American culture, the New

England weather, and the workload were hard enough. He discovered that his medical doctor wife, Jazz, couldn't work in Connecticut, so she had to live and work hundreds of miles away so they could make ends meet. During that first semester, his mother's cancer worsened. He couldn't afford a surprise trip to Manila, so when she died, he couldn't see her, or say good-bye or "I love you" one last time. As I have done many times, he cried by himself at night. During the summer break, at home in Manila, he decided that he never wanted to return to New Haven. It didn't matter that he had a full scholarship and was one of a few Filipinos to study at Yale. It was just too hard. He couldn't do it.

"Then," Melo said, "I remembered your invitations to the dinners at your house. And I knew that I belonged. I knew that I wasn't alone, and that gave me the strength to come back." I didn't know that when he invited me to lunch that day, he had done so because he was graduating the next month, and he wanted me to know that I had changed his whole life. The act of creating community can look simple, even mundane. But it can also be life changing. We weren't just making dinners. We were creating deep relationships that serve, support, and heal.

Changes Are Afoot

One thing I learned in my religious studies is that our experience of community has changed in a single generation. The number of people who say that they have no one to talk to about difficult subjects has tripled in the last few decades. Moreover, the size of the average person's social network decreased by one-third in the same time.[2] In fact, more people say that they don't have a confidante than those who say that they do.[3] Americans, particularly those under thirty, are not participating in formal religious organizations as much as people did even a generation ago. These religious organizations were often the basis for communities of values. According to a 2012 Pew Research report, "one-fifth of the US public—and a third of adults under 30—are religiously unaffiliated today, the highest percentages ever in Pew Research Center polling."[4] In addition, about three-quarters (74 percent) of these unaffiliated adults were raised with some affiliation, but have chosen to lapse. The statistics do not indicate that Americans think any differently about God or spirituality. On the contrary, overwhelming majorities continue to say that God and spirituality are important.[5]

Churches aren't the only social institutions to erode. In the 1970s almost two-thirds of Americans attended some kind of club meeting.[6] By the late 1990s nearly two-thirds had never attended a club meeting. The average American invested about a third less time in organizational life (excluding religious groups) in the thirty years from 1965 to 1995.[7] Even the number of picnics per capita went down 60 percent from 1975 to 1999![8]

Hunger for Connection and Community

The millennial generation may be more interested in connection and values-based activism than prior generations. They may be desperate for deeper connection, without the stale organizational baggage abandoned from a generation ago. Millennials prefer to live in dense, diverse urban villages where social interaction is closer than in isolated suburbs.[9] They're more likely to join a cause (environmental, social, economic, etc.) than a social club.[10] Millennials also want to make a difference in their communities: "High school seniors today are more likely than previous generations to state that making a contribution to society is very important to them and that they want to be leaders in their communities."[11] Consistent with this, 84 percent made a donation to charity in 2014.[12]

We know that social relationships have profound positive effects on our physical and mental health, longevity, and happiness. Loneliness kills, and the quality of our relationships matter. The seventy-five-year Study of Adult Development indicates that good relationships keep us happier and healthier. People who are socially disconnected are less happy, experience health declines earlier, and live shorter lives than people who are not lonely. One in five Americans report that they are lonely.[13] A 2010 review involving over 300,000 participants concluded that having weak social ties was as harmful to health as alcoholism! In fact, "a lack of social relationships was equivalent to smoking up to 15 cigarettes a day."[14]

The research indicates that Americans today are seeking connection with others who share their values. But they're not involved in communities that typically provide deep ongoing connection, membership, and life-honoring rituals. Best-selling author and marketing guru Seth Godin writes that people today want connection more than material things. He believes that we're in a connection economy in which those who connect others will succeed.[15]

When we do find people who share at least some of our values, there's a real opportunity for friendship. It doesn't matter if this is at work or on our block, or while volunteering in a distant country. Building community creates a venue for friendship, and friendship defeats loneliness. In deep community we can be vulnerable and still know that we belong. Those of us who are able to connect what may be a new lonely generation will have a profound effect on the health and well-being of those we serve no matter why we bring people together. I unwittingly started this journey because I was desperate to find a community for me. I promise you that I continue because I've learned how important it is for us all to know that we belong. The leaders who create this, well, we will change the world. I hope this inspires you.

Godspeed.
Charles H. Vogl
Oakland, California
CharlesVogl.com

Barnes & Noble Booksellers #1907
2900 Peachtree Road NE Suite 310
Atlanta, GA 30305
404-261-7747

STR:1907 REG:CO3 TRN:4227 CSHR:Katherine W

BUY ONLINE PICK UP IN STORE
ORDER NUMBER: 4093309200

The Art of Community: Seven Principles f
978 1626563419
                                Qty :   1
Total # of Items Picked Up: 1
BOPIS Tender CC 751T   20.64

Connect with us on Social

Facebook- @BNbuckhead
Instagram- @buckheadbn
Twitter- @BuckheadBN

053.01A   04/13/2020 02:27PM

CUSTOMER COPY

Items purchased as part of a Buy One Get One or Buy Two, Get Third Free offer are available for exchange only, unless all items purchased as part of the offer are returned, in which case such items are available for a refund (in 30 days). Exchanges of the items sold at no cost are available only for items of equal or lesser value than the original cost of such item.

Opened music CDs, DVDs, vinyl records, electronics, toys/games, and audio books may not be returned, and can be exchanged only for the same product and only if defective. NOOKs purchased from other retailers or sellers are returnable only to the retailer or seller from which they were purchased pursuant to such retailer's or seller's return policy. Magazines, newspapers, eBooks, digital downloads, and used books are not returnable or exchangeable. Defective NOOKs may be exchanged at the store in accordance with the applicable warranty.

Returns or exchanges will not be permitted (i) after 30 days or without receipt or (ii) for product not carried by Barnes & Noble.com, (iii) for purchases made with a check less than 7 days prior to the date of return.

Policy on receipt may appear in two sections.

Return Policy

With a sales receipt or Barnes & Noble.com packing slip, a full refund in the original form of payment will be issued from any Barnes & Noble Booksellers store for returns of new and unread books, and unopened and undamaged music CDs, DVDs, vinyl records, electronics, toys/games and audio books made within 30 days of purchase from a Barnes & Noble Booksellers store or Barnes & Noble.com with the below exceptions:

Undamaged NOOKs purchased from any Barnes & Noble Booksellers store or from Barnes & Noble.com may be returned within 14 days when accompanied with a sales receipt or with a Barnes & Noble.com packing slip or may be exchanged within 30 days with a gift receipt.

Introduction

The Inspiration for This Book

One sunny day in June, I sat in a bustling downtown San Francisco taqueria with Kevin Lin, a cofounder and chief operating officer of Twitch. Kevin oversees a billion-dollar online gaming brand that each month attracts tens of millions of visitors. Over a tostada and iced tea, he told me how his user numbers continue to explode. In just three years, his brand had almost accidentally created a meeting place for people who love video games.

To Kevin, it had become clear that users desperately wanted to be part of a community that represented their identity, values, and shared interests. The company had recently invited one thousand of these users to "partner" with the brand. They were extended privileges to work with the company in a special way that gave them a higher profile. Kevin shared that some people were so moved by the invitation that they cried. He knew that it had little to do with the financial opportunity—these users had already shown that they would provide content for free. What moved them was the sense that they were being welcomed somewhere and appreciated for who they were.

Many Twitch users felt misunderstood, unappreciated, and disconnected from the offline world, Kevin said, referring to the stigma of being a video game enthusiast. Just by the hours spent online at Twitch, they had already demonstrated how much they appreciated finding one another. But Kevin didn't know how to transform the group into a strong community: all he really knew to do was to invite them to visit and use the website. In fact, no one in his company knew time-tested principles for building a robust community endowed with a rich feeling of connection. Moreover, Twitch's leadership was reluctant to take risky steps to organize the users, lest such decisions ruin whatever was currently working. There were so many ideas I wanted to share with Kevin right away so that he and his team could better serve millions worldwide and make them feel more connected. He shared his vision for bigger live events around the world and a more harmonious global community.

This book is my offering to Kevin* and all the other community builders who are creating spaces where we can learn to be connected, defeat loneliness, and enrich lives by understanding where and how we belong. In short, this book is a tool for bringing friendship and support where there has been loneliness, fear, and separation. May your communities serve members in all the ways they are hungry to experience.

You probably already understand that it's important to belong to strong communities. They make us more effective in reaching goals and overcoming challenges large and small. Communities are created when at least two people begin to feel concern for each other's welfare. If others join this tiny caring flame, the community fire grows. This is as true for neighbors as for global activists and coworkers (or even competitors) taking on a big challenge. I designed this book to help current and future leaders working either in person or online to understand how to make their communi-

---

* To protect identities, I've changed the names and identifying details about other people in this book. They are all real people.

ties feel more connected, durable, and fulfilling. If it's successful, then your communities will do at least four things better. First, it'll help members grow in the ways they hope to. This growth can be technical, social, or internal. Second, it'll cause members to feel more connected, welcome, proud, and excited to be a part of the group. Third, it'll help members work together toward making the difference that you envision. Fourth, it'll make membership more fun.

Shared Values

For the purposes of this book, tribes are people who share certain values even if they're in different places or aren't connected yet. These values may show up in shared interests, activities, or life choices. Tribes want to be connected. They want to be around people who understand them. For example, there are many people in the world who value building confidence and courage in girls and are willing to take action. They create a tribe even if they haven't come together in a formal community like the Girl Scouts organization. The people who bring a tribe together to create a community are tribal leaders. Since you're reading this book, you're likely a tribal leader. Or maybe you're a tribal leader but haven't realized it yet. If so, you may be far more important to other people than you know.

Building Mature Communities

Your community may be very small; in fact, it might not even have begun yet. You may notice that your community uses almost none of the principles discussed in this book. *There's nothing wrong with this.* Small, informal communities can offer a lot of value with very little structure or consideration of what makes the community work. It's also possible that the principles are there, but you haven't been looking for them. Chances are, you're taking on one of two challenges. The first possibility is that you want to build or grow a community. This could consist of a group of students, tech workers, teachers, healers, advisers, or any other tribe with an interest in connecting with and caring about those around them. Communities can be formal, with official membership and administration (like Doctors Without Borders), or informal, tied by shared values and commitments (such as jungle bush pilots).

The second possibility is that you believe an existing community has the potential to become more connected or effective. The current community might look successful on the outside. You might even have lots of members, events, and funding. But communities that look strong and healthy are sometimes poorly organized. Many do not have a clear vision about what they do or where they're headed. They don't know how to make their activities more sophisticated, effective, or rewarding. They may not know how to connect newer members in a meaningful way with current members. And they may have trouble finding the right prospective members and helping them get involved. Right now, I'm working with a famous legacy church in San Francisco. More than two thousand people attend services there on Sundays. It looks strong, but I know that it's a real challenge to get younger members involved and to give visitors a clear way to connect with active members. While there's a lot happening at this church, its long-term sustainability is far from certain.

If you're not facing either of these challenges, don't worry: there's plenty for you to get from reading this book now. It can help you understand your current communities and the leadership style within them. You may be outside a community trying to understand it, either because you think you want to join it or because you're sure that you don't. Or maybe you're a leader who hasn't known that you've been waiting for these insights, and it may make your efforts far more powerful.

Crafting Community

I titled this book *The Art of Community* because the best community building is an art. There's no single formula. What works for you and your members will not work for everyone. Success will reflect your values, priorities, and growth. Just as in art, there are forms and skills you can build on, but copying someone else won't create something truly inspiring. You have to bring your own creativity and experience to the work. And while you must craft your own community, once you finish this book you'll see that there are seven core principles to community building that have served people for millennia. Even when an organization considers itself informal and unstructured, as it matures, these principles will appear—whether the members notice or not.

Serving Members

To create something that others want to join and support, we have to remember a core tenet: communities function best and are most durable when they're helping members to be more successful in some way in a connected and dynamic world. If you forget this, or even worse, if you never understand this, then your efforts will be misplaced. The communities I'm encouraging you to build should make people (including you) stronger, happier, and full of well-being. Simply gathering people on your block together can do this. So can connecting millions of people around the world. If we fail to get members excited about committing their time and effort, they'll leave.

Ego versus Good Community Leadership

One word of caution before we begin. You've probably been part of an exclusive group in which someone (or several someones) believed that, since they belonged to this particular group, they had permission to bask in their own achievements and mistreat more junior members. I hope that you saw how quickly that attitude erodes respect and influence. We will discuss "inner rings" in great detail in chapter 8. Leaders must set an example for senior members to respect and serve new members. Without this, some will certainly build up their own egos by disrespecting new members. They'll forget that the community is strongest when it attracts and supports like-valued people. Abusing new members will show that the community is a self-serving, self-aggrandizing, and potentially dangerous organization. It'll be dangerous because it'll be far more committed to serving its own needs than to serving as a supportive part of a healthy world.

Lastly, you may have visited or joined a community (formal or informal) that seemed great in the beginning, and then your interest waned. Maybe you got upset by the way it was run. Was it because it stopped helping you be who you wanted to be? Did it become just another chore or responsibility? Perhaps the community did a bad job of explaining what its true purpose was. You joined thinking that you would find help to achieve X, only to discover that the community was really focused on helping members achieve Y. If you had understood that at the outset, you would never have joined. Sometimes, as leaders bringing people together, we find it easy to become convinced of our own greatness. We can help avoid this by remembering that we can lead for the long term only when we're serving others.

Let's begin the cool stuff.

Part One

Recognizing Community

One

Understanding Community

In this book, I define a community as *a group of individuals who share a mutual concern for one another's welfare.* It's distinct from a group whose members may share ideas, interests, proximity, or any number of things but lack concern for one another. Such groups can have huge memberships, like the Museum of Modern Art, the American Medical Association, or Greenpeace, but their members do not share any strong social connectedness. Robert Putnam, a political scientist at Harvard, says it best: "They root for the same team and they share some of the same interests, but they are unaware of each other's existence. Their ties, in short, are to common symbols, common leaders, and perhaps common ideals, but not to one another."[1]

When we see that others are concerned about our own welfare, we'll invest more in building community with them, and we'll feel more connected. We have communities in our lives that don't have formal membership but to which we feel connected because of this perceived mutual concern: the neighbors on your street or in your apartment building, your pickup sports friends, or even the people you know from your commute. Though informal, these are real and important communities.

Recognizing a Community

There are certain features that are almost universal in healthy communities. While communities have different levels of maturation and sophistication, these features will quickly emerge as communities mature and gain importance. Your success in growing a community will depend on how well you can understand and articulate the following features:

Shared values
Membership identity
Moral proscriptions
Insider understanding

Values Bind a Community

We all want to be part of a group of people who share our values. It doesn't matter if we dress, behave, work, or consume similarly, or even whether we live in the same area. We want to believe that others value what we value (and disdain what we disdain). Shared values are what attract us to a group in the first place. By understanding how a group develops and expresses values, a leader can help a community mature and grow.

We may seek out a community because of a shared activity or interest (people sharing interests often share behaviors). Shared activity indicates sharing *some* value for the activity. But we'll feel disconnected from such a community if we discover that there aren't enough shared values. For example, consider CrossFit Oakland (CFO). It's a fitness training facility and an affiliate of the global CrossFit fitness network known for a particular style of high-intensity workouts. The CrossFit company that created the network was founded in Northern California in 2000 by Greg Glassman and Lauren Jenai.[2] There are now over thirteen thousand affiliate gyms and more than two million exercisers in the network around the world.[3] The gyms are famous for their strong cultural identity, which includes creating supportive communities that help women get strong alongside men.[4]

CFO is a local gym founded by Mike Minium. He knows that members may *join* because the gym offers high-intensity and varied training, but they *stay* because they feel connected and welcome. The community values health, safety, and respect for personal growth far more than strength, speed, and competitiveness. Members show it in their words and instruction and in their acceptance of people at all levels of physical ability. If you look at CFO's website, you'll find this language (edited):

> We believe in working hard so you can play outside, play inside, play with your kids, play with your friends, play on vacation, and play your way through life.
>
> We do what we do because we believe it works to get you fitter, stronger, and healthier.
>
> We believe it empowers you to perform better in the gym, in sport, and in life.
>
> We do what we do so that more of you can live longer, healthier, happier, more amazing lives.
>
> We serve you if you want to get in shape and don't know where to begin.
>
> We serve you if you are looking to get better (faster, stronger, fitter) at your sport.
>
> We serve you if you are looking for real, tangible, and lasting changes in your overall health and appearance.
>
> We serve you if you are seeking quality coaching and a supportive community.

It may surprise you that there's belief and service language on a website for a fitness center. I discuss this later. For now, you can see how their public language clearly shares that they value faster, stronger, and healthier members. They also value community, health, and those who "don't know where to begin" (novices). I know from conversations with Mike and from personal visits to CFO gyms that there are also unstated values in the community around honoring the effort of those with the most physical challenges. These include safety, patience, and long-term health rather than near-term performance. Anyone who can afford the fees at CFO can join. But only those who embrace the stated and unstated values will connect and feel genuinely welcome. CFO is a community because the members don't just train together, they care for one another. And members will stay only as long as they continue to feel CFO's commitment to those values.

Virtually all communities express their values either consciously or unconsciously, and often in both ways. They do it with actions and with words. Visitors can learn about these values in explicit ways on a website, in marketing materials, and from formal inquiry. But implicit ways are *at least* as powerful. They include what members say to one another, whom they welcome, what they share, and with whom and where they spend their money. No matter what the explicit values are, the implicit values will reveal the real deal.

My favorite way is to see where they put their "warm body." I look for what community members value so much that they actually put their bodies near it. With CFO, for example, leaders and members spend significant time in the gym, greet new visitors in person, and help new or low-performing athletes with their exercises rather than spending their time only with high performers. Where members put their warm bodies tells a visitor whether they mean what they say. You may know groups that say they value generosity, contribution, and cooperation, but you have seen that they're actually selfish. Most people quickly figure out the truth.

When I was a documentary filmmaker in New York City, I felt closely connected to an informal community of social justice filmmakers. There was no official membership card or secret handshake. Most of us belonged to several film organizations, but membership in them was not required to be part of our community. Even though there was no formal membership, I felt connected because I knew that other filmmakers cared about my success and well-being, just as I cared about theirs. We shared equipment, crew, legal knowledge, our own labor, and many hard-won lessons. When the film-making partner of one of our members was kidnapped in Nigeria, we raised money to pay for his safe return and provided much-needed emotional support.

I was attracted to that community because we valued telling important stories that would bring a measure of justice and healing to the world. We valued spending our time and money to tell stories that might never provide a positive return on the financial investments we made. We all valued making a difference in the world far more than our own comfort. To this day, I am proud to be a social change documentary filmmaker. Understanding the shared values that attract and keep members in a community is important for leaders. For continued success, leaders must both clearly share and personally represent the values so others can recognize what they want to join.

A community's values evolve as times and people change. Your community almost certainly values something more than outsiders do. It's not important that on the first day you can recognize and name the ultimate values for your community. In fact, it may take some time to understand what things you value more than others. Moreover, as time passes and culture changes, it's imperative that the community values also change. This is how you stay relevant in a dynamic world. For example, it was not long ago that many American communities (like churches) valued racial segregation. While this is still a value in some places, a lot has changed since the 1950s.

Formalization can destroy a community if values are ignored. When efforts arise to formalize or corporatize a community, there's often understandable concern that the effort could destroy the very community it seeks to grow. This is why it's so important to recognize *both* the explicit and the implicit values that attract and keep members connected. Remember how CFO explicitly values higher performance and a supportive community, and how it implicitly values patience and the efforts of low-performing athletes. Any effort to grow will fail if members sense that the community leadership is neglecting important values or introducing unwelcome ones. For-profit corporations are particularly at risk for this if they value members for their revenue potential rather than for their contribution and commitment. Leaving any meaningful portion of core members feeling disconnected or abandoned is a real danger when formalizing or corporatizing a community and can lead to its destruction.

My friend Margaret has been working for years at a well-known ski resort I'll call Ski Valley. She told me what happened when a major corporate resort operator took over. The new owners celebrated the "soul" of the resort in their marketing, but their actions eroded the connections, camaraderie, and commitment the employees felt at work. She described how she and her coworkers used to look out for one another. She valued the connection between work lives and social lives, the freedom to improve the operations, and the friendliness of a workplace built for happiness.

That all changed when the corporate leadership came. The Welcome sign at the lodge entrance was replaced with three new signs: No Dogs, No Alcohol, and No Drones. Instead of each department celebrating its holiday parties as it chose, all were invited to a combined fifteen-hundred-person event with no intimacy. Now, instead of being able to knock on a manager's door or chat in the locker room to discuss operational improvements, staff receive instructions come from someone miles away. Not only does Margaret miss the opportunity to discuss improvements, she doesn't even know the name of the decision maker. The values that she appreciated about the community aren't there anymore. Margaret said that employees who were fundamentally "do gooders" have left. Instead of coming to work excited to improve guest experiences, many others just "show up." I suspect that whatever standards the executives wanted to bring in, they didn't plan to destroy a culture of vigilant improvement and mutual support.

Communities can have unhealthy implicit values (without knowing it). Unhealthy values are those that aren't serving members and may even restrict connection and enrichment. You've probably seen this in a community somewhere. I briefly worked at an elite educational institution where there was an implicit value of demonstrating "effortless brilliance." Some seemed to love this and showed off their mastery by dazzling others. But many students felt oppressed, fearful, and trapped by this value. They weren't confident that they had brilliance to share. Often, they wouldn't say *anything* aloud for fear that someone else would cut them down and thus demonstrate a greater effortless brilliance.

You can imagine how little social connection and enrichment was fostered when students feared speaking. The problem was so severe that several students I knew created their own secret communities to be safe from the inevitable criticism and judgment of their peers. In particular, spiritual and religious communities often run into this challenge of unwelcoming implicit values. They may advocate an explicit value of welcoming strangers, but their language (and whom they stand next to) shows that they value their own homogeneity, familiarity, and conformity. It's largely the disagreement over values and apparent hypocrisy that angers outsiders and prevents visitors from joining for connection.

Values and Membership Identity

Because members share values, the community helps answer three important questions for members in some way:

Who am I?
How should I act?
What do I believe?

I call this *membership identity*. The identity may not apply to all areas of a person's life. In fact, to an outsider it may appear that the values and identities are inconsistent with other areas in the person's life. For example, someone can be generous and kind in one community (church, poker group, or alumni association) and a selfish bully everywhere else. You've probably seen this kind of compartmentalized identity.

What's important to understand is that when a member is in the community, the community's values and identity feel comfortable and right. Further, when members are around other members, those values and their identity are reinforced. Obviously, the particular values and identities that are reinforced will have profoundly different influences in different people's lives. Some values and identities are deeply helpful and others equally hurtful. As a shorthand here, I'll define healthy values as those that encourage members to care for and enrich themselves and others. The more broadly that care is defined, the better.

Stop here for a moment, and think: how would you describe your community's membership identity? If your response is that your community doesn't tell members who they are, what they should do, or what they should believe about anything at any level, then there are two possibilities. First, you're not really creating a community, but only a group. A group may share interests and values, but a community has connections so that members care for the welfare of one another. Second, you're simply not recognizing the membership identity. Consider why someone would seek you out and what that person hopes to gain as a member. Consider what that person expects of members and leadership, both formal and informal.

For example, if you have a weekend bicycling community, are there ideals that your members hold about bicycling? Perhaps they enjoy biking because it's good for their health, or because it's for the brave and adventurous, or because it's an environmentally friendly outdoor activity. These provide an outline for your community's identity. Does your community have ideas about how good bicyclists act? (This is usually identified by contrasting with how bad bicyclists act.) Do you have ideas about your identity as bicyclists? Do you welcome anyone with a bicycle? At any age or skill level? Will someone preparing for the Tour de France fit in with this community? How about a ten-year-old with a mountain bike? You might answer that anyone who enjoys bicycling is welcome, that you have special events for beginners, others for racers, and others for off-roaders. But would a bicycling police officer recording your group for terrorist surveillance fit in equally well?

The point of these questions is to help you recognize that there may be identities present in your community that are unrecognized and unstated. It's important for you to consider them carefully, because there's a twofold danger to not recognizing them. Below are examples shared with me from people I know within supportive communities they cherish.

Melissa recently retired as the first female firefighter captain in the history of New Haven, Connecticut. In her career she ran the busiest firehouse in the city and oversaw two teams. Over the years she has pulled people out of wrecked cars, responded to shootings, and of course put out fires. She told me that she absolutely has a community of firefighters that she knows will respond to her no matter the hour, weather, or emergency. They know that she'll do the same for them. Here's how she describes the identity of her personal community of firefighters:

Melissa's Firefighter Community

Values

Being hypervigilant about saving lives, including a willingness to take high risks.

Embracing life in the present.

Training for years for the single worst day of someone's life.

Deep understanding about a place and circumstances to be ready for emergencies ("pre-fire planning").

Identity

Who I am: I'm the fixer on the worst days. I'm the assurance in terrible circumstances.

How I should act: I show up no matter how bad or uncontrollable the situation. I exude confidence and control no matter what surprises show up.

What I believe: I believe life is fragile. I believe our lives can change in a moment, and I believe risking my life is worth saving someone else.

Adam is an executive chef in the San Francisco Bay Area who runs professional kitchens and consults for restaurant owners. He's also building a national food company. He has a community of executive chefs who support one another with big events and logistical challenges, and celebrate together with lots of food. Here's how he describes the identity of his community of chefs:

Adam's Executive Chef Community

Values

Working long hours to create excellent food.

Creating new food experiences.

Respecting people who make extraordinary food.

Identity

Who I am: I am an authority on culinary methods and responsible for making thousands of meals excellent every time.

How I should act: I learn about new food research, flavors, and ingredients. I find better ways to solve cooking problems, improve food, and support other chefs when they need help.

What I believe: Feeding people is important and worth long hours to do well. Food is exciting and makes the lives of others better.

Sara is a film director and producer. For over ten years she's worked in both New York and San Francisco on projects that air on network television and national PBS, and tour the world in film festivals. She's a part of a documentary film community that shares equipment, shares labor on projects, and helps one another navigate the changing media funding and legal landscape. Here's how she describes the identity of her filmmaking community:

Sara's Filmmaker Community

Values

Understanding someone else's viewpoint.

Dispelling stereotypes and prejudices.

Sharing the truth no matter how uncomfortable.

Creating empathy for people and ideas that are unknown or misunderstood.

Identity

Who I am: I'm a storyteller who hopes to share true nuance about people and create empathy.

How I should act: I seek out people whose stories are unknown or misrepresented and share them to contribute to understanding the world.

What I believe: I believe everyone has a voice and not everyone has the tools to project their voice. I believe it is my responsibility to get more voices heard. I believe that sharing the truth in powerful, visual ways can make a difference in people's lives.

To grow a tight community, it's essential to articulate the community's core values clearly, at least for yourself. Not every value needs to be articulated, just the most important ones: those that tie the community's members together. There are values that someone must share to be a functioning community member. Can you be a functioning part of a supportive chef community if you don't value cooking? What if you don't value quality?

When we can speak of the core values, then we have principles that can be used to evaluate options for the community. We can ask: "Will this decision help us build on our core values?" It's possible that something grows without the values named, but then it becomes difficult to know if new ideas and options will grow in a way that serves and strengthens.

For example, Kevin's online gaming community has grown far larger than he ever expected. He had thought that there might be hundreds who would want to join, but its membership is now in the tens of millions. He wonders how leadership can invest in strengthening the community without destroying what makes it great in its current form. I don't know what's best; I'm not part of this community. But I do know that the community will appreciate investments that support its core values.

There are many things the community can or does value, including these:

Performance
Improving gaming skills
Learning about new technology
Influencing game development
Proving who's the best

Connection
Connecting with other gamers
Creating local and online friendships

Entertainment
Finding inexpensive entertainment

Dignity
Improving perceptions of online gamers
Gaining legitimacy in the worldwide sports community

The first thing Kevin needs to do is to *talk with the community*. By doing so, he'll learn more about what values matter to the members. This particular community is old enough and large enough that there are now subcommunities, and they may have slightly different values.

I hope you can see why Kevin should start by fully understanding and articulating the core values he intends to strengthen. If he simply dives in, for example, by starting a program to help gamers improve their skills, this could be a wasted investment, or even a disaster, if the community's real core value is connecting gamers with one another. Conversely, if he invests in social features to improve connection, but members are there to acquire better skills from experts, the new features could feel silly, distracting, and foreign.

If you don't know the values, you may not know who's seeking you. You may even seek out people with the wrong values and beliefs. This is no good if you intend to strengthen your existing community with more members who share the current values. I remember speaking to a martial arts school entrepreneur who explained to me that martial arts schools often fail because instructors assume members value fighting, self-defense, and discipline. But the reality is that many martial arts students simply value a fun way to stay fit. They're casual athletes, not fighters.

You may expect and ask members to do things that disregard their values. This is one way that efforts to formalize a community can destroy it. If members understand that these efforts fit with their values and identities, they'll be enthusiastic about incorporating the new structures. But if not, you risk alienating your core members. I know a training director who rushed volunteer leadership trainers to compress hours of material into minutes. He valued lots of material presented quickly. The trainers and students valued interactive learning far more. Within days, all the trainers and participants abandoned the curriculum.

Behavior often precedes adopting common values. The importance of understanding that core values are different from common values becomes clear when we understand their relationship to behavior. Visitors should be aware of core values before they explore membership, but they don't have to embrace all the common values of the group.

For a rapidly expanding community, it's critical that prospective members are welcome to participate in community behavior before adopting common values. Visitors can have general interest or prefer to experience something before commitment. This is an idea that many religious and spiritual communities misunderstand. Few want to join a community where they must adopt an overwhelming number of life-changing values before they can participate at any level. Can you imagine visiting a bicycling club if the first thing you had to do was profess five required lifestyle-changing values about bicycling? (Bicycling can change values about eating, stretching, getting outdoors, etc.) Another way to say the same thing is that for members, while there may be early interest, behavior often comes first, and adopting values can come later with experience.

While some values are core and required, other values are simply common among members. After participation, if prospective members reject core values, they'll leave the community on their own. (In fact, if the core values are made clear enough at the outset, the prospective member may decline to participate.) It's important that new members be given time and flexibility in adopting values. When I lived in New Haven, Connecticut, I started a contemplative prayer group. When I founded the group, I thought that it wouldn't matter whether members had specific ideas about God's nature, kept a particular relationship with God, or even were confident about the existence of God. I wanted to include anyone with an interest in our discussions and contemplative prayer.

We had one participant who really enjoyed being part of the prayer group, but it soon became clear that he was more interested in philosophy than in theology. His own dismissal of God's existence left no room to develop conversations about understanding God at any level. I had to determine what our group's core values were: What would allow us to create a safe space for the members we sought out? It was important that members valued contemplative prayer, broadly defined, and thought it could enrich their lives. It was also important that members valued sharing and listening to each other's thoughts about their experience of God.

It was difficult for me to contemplate restricting membership. But when I considered what kind of community I wanted to create, I had to acknowledge that a core value was respecting and honoring others as they shared their thoughts about God. It wasn't important that someone share my particular beliefs about God. If I had communicated that core value up front, my friend would have realized early on that this was not a community for him. Or he could have participated, learned how our core value led to theological conversations (behavior), and then chosen whether to join, based perhaps on his value changing. Maybe seeing us seek out contemplative prayer would grow new interest in him. Maybe.

I was missing two things. The first was clarity on what were critical core values for the group, and the second was differing rings, one for outsiders to visit and one for insiders to share a protected space. For example, after firefighter recruits live and work in a firehouse for a year, they learn to appreciate (value) with deep respect both the trust and commitment of their crewmates. They also learn to support crewmates outside work with life's challenges. These values make people better firefighters. Fine dining cooks usually spend a year in a high-performing kitchen before they value taking time to make food right and maximizing ingredient use. Orchestra musicians value the role of music in their lives. Once members play in an orchestra, they learn to value breathing together in preparation. They learn to value creating a magnificent sound texture rather than standing out as an exceptional musician.

The critical lesson here is that prospective members must have a way to behave like the current community members (participate) before we require them to believe in and value the same things we do (no matter how trivial or significant). When we understand this, we can find a way to both respect our community values and acknowledge that newcomers may need time to grow into full membership.

Communities and Moral Proscriptions

A community provides moral proscriptions on how members should behave and treat others. The community may not provide proscriptions for *all* areas of morality, but it will for those areas that relate to the community's core values. The morals may be unidentified, seldom discussed, or unacknowledged, but you'll see them clearly if you ask these questions:

> What and whom do we protect?
> What is intolerable?
> What do we share?
> With whom do we share?
> Whom do we respect?
> How do we show respect?

When you think of communities that have fallen apart or eroded, you may think of activities that betrayed the community's values and moral prescriptions, whether or not the values or moral prescriptions were clearly articulated. For example, the revelations of child abuse in the Catholic Church eroded respect for the church not only because children were abused but also because perpetrators were apparently protected and justice for the victims denied. This is opposed to the church's stated values of serving all church members and honoring justice.

If your group does anything together or supports members in participating in any activity, it's almost certain that the community advocates certain moral proscriptions. For example, even in a bicycling group there are proscriptions on how morally responsible bicyclists (us!) behave in contrast to others (them!). How restrictive the proscriptions are depends on the community. Many leaders do not recognize that their communities offer moral proscriptions. It sounds too restrictive. But even violent criminal gangs have moral proscriptions about behavior. These influence how members honor one another, their leaders, and others important to the community. A member who violates those proscriptions risks being expelled from the gang, and perhaps much worse. As a leader, you may never need to write out standards for community behavior (moral proscriptions). But a time may come when they need to be articulated. Don't be afraid. Such standards are what define strong communities. As long as the proscriptions truly reflect the shared values of your community, members will be enthusiastic about them. Communities provide moral proscriptions consistent with their values.

Communities and Insider Understandings

One of the great pleasures of being part of a community is that we don't have to explain ourselves. We want to feel seen and understood without explaining the parts that outsiders don't get. We feel more comfortable and safer within the community because of this baseline understanding. In the outside world, it may be less clear that we and our values are understood and accepted. Part of our comfort comes with technical or "external" understanding. This is how insiders understand the external world. We don't want to explain terms or recap history and the fundamentals of our field. We want to come together and share our values and skills.

Recently my friend Kari returned home to Oregon and gathered with friends who have a long history of playing jazz together. One musician came with a friend who was a musician but not a jazz musician, and who hadn't brought an instrument. She didn't share the jazz tradition, so she politely sat to the side as the group of six played. Kari told me that instead of playing for two to three hours, as they had in the past, they played for only thirty minutes, largely because they were uncomfortable playing with an outsider sitting idly by who didn't appreciate jazz very much. While everyone had good intentions, inviting an outsider who had neither the technical knowledge nor the musical interest for this special time changed the space and eroded the intimacy of the community time.

Perhaps the more important part of insider understanding is the emotional or "internal" understanding. This is understanding about how it feels for insiders and the values that drive choices no matter how hard, easy, fun, painful, scary, or noble it looks to outsiders. For example, in Weight Watchers communities, there's confidence that members understand and value the struggle required to maintain a healthy body weight. Firefighters understand both what experiences are dangerous and why they are so, and they share the emotional reality of living through them. They also understand the love of the job that comes from saving people in life-threatening situations. In communities where patients with similar diagnoses and challenges connect, they feel enormous relief that everyone in the room or conversation understands the fears, challenges, discomfort, and elation that comes with their own journey.

My favorite example comes from my retired firefighter friend, Melissa, who explained to me that her colleagues have a dark sense of humor that may come from regular exposure to mortal challenges. The humor is a kind of release for them. Even when the firefighters' spouses are present, the conversation is not as comfortable and the language is not as free. She knows that with firefighters she can say things that would be jarring to outsiders yet respectful to crewmates who share her experience.

I'm hopeful that these past few pages have opened some insight into how and why the communities you already cherish stick together. You may have seen something new that means you can articulate something that has previously remained unsaid. This may be something your community already values or an understanding you share. In naming it, you may gain clarity on why you are together and understand who is looking for you so they can grow what you've started. Whatever you grow, it will stand on this originating core of identity.

Part Two

Seven Principles
for Belonging

The Seven Principles

Part Two presents the seven principles that any tribal leader can implement in a growing or emerging community. You may notice that communities you value already use some or all of these principles even though you may not have recognized it before. Some principles may sound surprising and unnecessary, but on further reflection you'll probably realize that these principles are already present, though perhaps undistinguished in your communities. The principles we will explore in detail are:

1. *Boundary*: The line between members and outsiders.
2. *Initiation*: The activities that mark a new member.
3. *Rituals*: The things we do that have meaning.
4. *Temple*: A place set aside to find our community.
5. *Stories*: What we share that allows others and ourselves to know our values.
6. *Symbols*: The things that represent ideas that are important to us.
7. *Inner Rings*: A path to growth as we participate.

It's not necessary that you apply all these principles to your community, and certainly not right away. Only fairly mature communities will have thought out and included all of them. They're simply presented as tools to use when you want to strengthen what you have at whatever level you're at today. I admire organizations like Weight Watchers, CrossFit, and Alcoholics Anonymous, all of whom exemplify many of these principles. They show how a secular, even for-profit enterprise can authentically bring together like-valued people to serve. As you read about the seven principles, you'll see both how they've already been employed in your favorite communities and how you can strengthen the way you use them. Ideally, finding ways to use these principles should be fun. Depending on what you've already grown, you may have members desperately waiting for you to use these principles and you don't even know it.

Two

The Boundary Principle

Members want to know who's in the community and shares their values. Visitors want to know a safe way to explore without committing themselves. Novices prefer to know at what point they've joined a community. A boundary is the recognized demarcation between insiders (members) and outsiders. This boundary should be more about making the inside space safe for insiders than about keeping outsiders out. Where there's a boundary, insiders feel more confident that they share values and that they understand one another better than outsiders.

For example, my friend Amanda belongs to a young mothers' group based in her hometown of Lowell, Massachusetts. There's an online forum they use to communicate on social media, and informal in-person gatherings when they see one another in town. Only moms are allowed. Amanda has shared how important this is to her, because she feels judged and scolded by strangers who comment on her choices as a mother. She believes only mothers can understand and empathize with the challenges she and her peers face with their young children. This means pediatricians, therapists, or even experienced nannies are not welcome unless they're also mothers. In this community, even fathers don't qualify because they don't share a mother's experience. Amanda has noticed that even mothers from a few years ago had different medical knowledge, parenting advice, and equipment available for their time. That creates a certain kind of empathy separation. It's important to her that when she shares her fears, challenges, and failures, she's safe from uninformed, dated, or insensitive judgment. The boundary is very important.

In monastic orders, the barriers to crossing the boundary can be high indeed. It often includes a novice period with several stages (postulate, novitiate, and juniorate). During this time, elders assess whether the novice can live according to the principles, values, and disciplines of the order. This process can take years. After successfully crossing the boundary, a member can be called a "life-professed" member with voting privileges. Boundaries like this are found in virtually all Christian monastic traditions, including Roman Catholic, Protestant, Anglican, Eastern Orthodox, and Eastern Rite. In Shamanic traditions all over the world, stepping onto the sacred path of priesthood requires students to be willing to lose everything in their lives in order to become something new. This can include family relationships, working roles, and belongings. To ensure that the community is welcoming to new members, there must be a clear route across the boundary for outsiders with shared values who want to join the community.

Without a boundary you'll face an everything–nothing conundrum. Some communities want to be open to anyone and everyone. This arises from a generous instinct: making a community open for all sounds welcoming. Most leaders, even if they claim to "welcome everyone," actually mean something a bit more restrictive. If everything in the universe is good (and nothing is not good), then good things can never be differentiated from anything else in the universe. Good then identifies no (particular) thing because all things are good. Likewise, if everyone in the world belongs in your community, this can mean your community cannot be distinguished from no community.

A community is defined by at least one or more values (maybe something as simple as valuing bicycling or living on your block). This value can often be *recognized* by an interest or activity. For example, my friend Bruce walks for over an hour each Friday night on the streets of East Oakland. He is part of Ceasefire Oakland. *Anyone can join.* But only certain people join him in perceived dangerous neighborhoods. These members are brought together by their value of showing the city that someone cares about creating peace through nonviolent presence.

Many leaders confuse self-selection (no invitation necessary) with "everyone belongs." If someone in the history of the world can or will be excluded from your community, then there's some difference between potential insiders and all outsiders. No matter how small the difference or how wide the welcome, the distinction (shared value) is important to identify so that future members can recognize it and understand that they belong inside. If you think of very strong communities, the kind that stand together even when facing death, the kind that spend their last resources to rescue a member in trouble or to travel great distances to support someone in need, whether monasteries, militaries, or families, these communities have a clear boundary where they know who's in and who's not.

You may already have an invisible boundary and authority. Often communities think that they have no boundaries or gatekeepers, but actually they do. Both the boundary and the gatekeepers may be informal and unarticulated. Still, most insiders know who has the authority to reject a potential member, or even expel an existing member, if that person is acting inappropriately or doesn't share the community's core values. Some communities deny the existence of this boundary or authority. But when asked, members can often recall an instance when someone was excluded (often for good reason), and it's then clear how the exclusion was enforced.

Many years ago, when I was living in New York, I was asked to help grow and formalize an Interspiritual community. *Interspiritual* refers to a tradition of learning from several different spiritual traditions to pursue faith inquiry. At an initial meeting that included participants from across the country, some members said that the group was for everyone no matter their beliefs, practices, traditions, or anything else.

While I was certain that they were sincere, I suspected that this was not entirely true. As I learned more about the history of the community, I learned that there was a time when a member advocated polyamory and polygamy, which was far too iconoclastic for most of the group. Many even feared that they would all be stigmatized because of that member's exuberance. After several conversations, he was asked not to participate, and he's no longer involved. When I pointed out that this looked like a clear example that not everyone belongs in the group, it started a conversation to name the boundary that was already there. It wasn't easy, especially since an hour earlier all had been convinced that no such boundary existed.

An exploration zone is important for visitors. This is how we protect insiders while giving outsiders a chance to participate, to learn more about our community, and to decide whether it's right for them. We can encourage explorers by sharing some specified activities and areas, but not all. These are outer ring activities. Areas reserved for insiders (whether formal or informal) are inner ring. The vast majority of activities can be outer ring. The larger the outer ring, the more outsiders can evaluate a community before seeking membership. It's important to have an inner ring, too, as this gives shared-values explorers something to aspire to and provides that important safe space for your members.

For example, my friend Adam, the executive chef in San Francisco, tells me that his community of upper-level chefs hosts dinners for friends (outer ring event), but at these dinners the kitchen is accessible only to the chefs (inner ring). They don't want to spend their evening explaining what they're doing or training amateur cooks. They have the privilege of using the kitchen. Sometimes newcomers who seem to share their values are also invited to other private dinners reserved only for the chefs (inner ring). Adam tells me that if newcomers contribute a dish that's uncreative or poorly prepared, they won't be invited back. The community wants only members who are excited by food and who can put in the time needed to create great food.

If you prefer welcoming visitors to *all* community activities, an inner ring can be designated by privileges (at these same events). This means that members are allowed to do things that visitors are not. These privileges might include the following:

Providing opening remarks

Inviting guests

Scheduling events

Reserving space

Teaching skills

By maintaining outer ring and inner ring differences, visitors can feel confident that they're in fact visiting without unintentionally becoming a member.

The boundary is maintained by either a formal or an informal authority. Think about the communities you value. Even if there's no formal authority structure, there's probably a person or group of persons who can exclude someone they think is dangerous. It's imperative that the boundary is protected according to *community values*, as opposed to personal preferences, petty concerns, or whimsical criteria. The boundary can be poorly protected in two ways. First, it can be overly inclusive, if people with mismatched values are permitted inside. In this case, members will feel unsafe. It will be difficult or impossible for them to share vulnerability and deep connections when members don't trust that all the other participants in the community share their core values. Second, it can be overly exclusive, if shared-values participants are excluded. In this case, questions will be raised as to what the true community values are and, even more specifically, where the authority really lies.

In regulating the boundary, it's important to recognize what unstated values are actually enforced in contrast with those that are outwardly stated. If authority swings away from value-based inclusion in either direction, at least two things can destroy a community: First, members will begin to doubt the community's true values, and their participation and membership will waver. Second, members will reject the authority's values and then the authority.

Because of these dangers, both explicit and implicit values must be discussed and prioritized. You may know that fairly recent analysis of admission data for Harvard University appears to indicate that a limit is placed on the number of Asian students admitted each year. The limits may be egregious. According to the *New York Times,* "In 2008, over half of all applications to Harvard with exceptionally high SAT scores were Asian, yet they made up only 17 percent of the entering class. Asians are the fastest growing racial group in America, but their proportion of Harvard undergraduates has been flat for two decades." Unfortunately, this resembles the blatantly racist admissions policies of the early twentieth century designed to limit the number of Jews at Harvard.[1]

The Harvard admissions website includes the following language: "We seek promising students who will contribute to the Harvard community during their college years, and to society throughout their lives." It describes a stated value of students who will contribute. Unfortunately, the admissions numbers indicate an additional unstated value of limiting Asian student access. As Yascha Mounk, who teaches at Harvard, wrote in the *New York Times*, "The real problem is that, in a meritocratic system, whites would be a minority—and Harvard just isn't comfortable with that."[2]

While I cannot know how right Mounk is about what makes Harvard comfortable or what causes the numbers, you can imagine that the cachet of this community could diminish when the boundaries are enforced by values that are unattractive or downright distasteful. How much will Harvard suffer if all understand that white admissions have been protected more than any other for at least one hundred years? Will some "society contributors" go elsewhere?

If members trust that the boundary is enforced according to explicitly stated values they embrace, they'll appreciate the enforcement. Maintaining this trust requires keeping the space safe from intruders *and* wholeheartedly welcoming shared-values outsiders.

Remember the Interspiritual group I mentioned earlier? When I learned that someone had been asked to leave, I inquired about who had done the asking. I was told that it was two leaders who themselves maintained that they were not leaders. One, Jim, is a formally trained Buddhist who has practiced that tradition for many years. He insisted that he was only a facilitator. But when I pointed out that he had the authority to ask a member to leave, the group had to reconsider whether there were boundary keepers and what authority they held. They understood that if I asked someone to leave the group, my request would not have the weight of authority that Jim's did.

Community values will mature over time as times and people change, just as values do for whole countries and generations. For a long time, social clubs in the United States preferred to keep their membership male and all white. In the twenty-first century, any social club with such values is immediately suspected of being old and stuck in the past, or worse. Unless they want to attract only racist and sexist people, such clubs will have difficulty attracting new members.

Values, boundary, and enforcement all must remain dynamic. This is how a community matures. If maturation stops, the community will gradually become irrelevant. You can probably think of communities that were once important and are now irrelevant or on the way out. A friend of mine joined the local chapter of a national men's group. They have secret knowledge to learn, secret rituals to complete, and even secret places to meet. My friend really likes the members of his group. He's also aware that many other chapters are desperate for members. They'll take anyone just to keep from dying out. This men's group is becoming irrelevant because it values all-male secret meetings in a time and place when that's far less valued than before. If the group doesn't adapt to our more gender-equal times, it may lose all relevance.

Gatekeepers are important for helping visitors across the boundary. They're the people who can give newcomers access to the community. Whether officially or unofficially, gatekeepers evaluate whether an interested newcomer should be welcomed across the boundary and into the community. They may be the same as or different from those who can exclude.

For example, imagine a choir that has a strong community (perceived concern for one another's welfare). It may be that anyone in the choir can invite people to audition, introduce them to leaders, and include them in social events (outer ring), while there may be only one or a few insiders who have the (informal or formal) authority to keep someone away. The gatekeeper here is the choirmaster, who will decide if this newcomer has the potential to be a strong singing voice and is welcomed to inner ring practices and performances.

In other communities there may be many gatekeepers, but if newcomers never meet one, they can't ever truly cross the boundary. This concept is important to understand because growing communities need to give newcomers access to gatekeepers. If there aren't gatekeepers, it'll become unclear how newcomers are evaluated, even if the evaluation is casual.

A friend I'll call Travis is a pastor at a large urban church that embraces radical inclusivity. We have talked for hours about how the church can grow to serve the next generation. The church is so famous that at least half of the two thousand–plus attendees each Sunday are visitors and tourists. The church has no problem sharing what it is, what it values, and how it should act.

However, both the leadership and I know that it's hard for visitors who want to get beyond just visiting to connect with the church community. While there's a simple membership card to fill out in the pews, it's not at all clear what happens next. I know people who became formal members but didn't know where to go or whom to contact to make personal connections. They volunteered at the church's meal program, but found that they were treated more as free labor than as people looking to connect with other church members. They left the volunteer experiences without anyone welcoming them to the church community or expressing any interest in knowing them better.

Imagine the attrition rate because visitors couldn't find a way in. Is this happening in the communities we're forming? My friend's church needs formal or informal gatekeepers who can be easily approached. Right now, visitors have to seek out the pastors to find out more about membership, and there are only three pastors. Gatekeepers could help give newcomers access by extending invitations as soon as visitors shared that they want more.

Three

The Initiation Principle

We all want to know that we're truly accepted into the communities we join. An initiation is any activity that's understood as official recognition and welcome into the community. The initiation helps members understand clearly who's part of the community. It marks the completed journey over the boundary and into the inner ring.

After the initiation, insiders gain new privileges and are valued for having crossed over the boundary. They have nothing more to prove. They feel confident and welcome in their belonging. Ideally, all insiders' names are known. All the world's major religions have many kinds of initiations that mark the transition to full membership. This includes recognition as a fully privileged adult member. Among the common and ancient initiations are Christian baptism, Jewish bar mitzvah and bat mitzvah, Hindu aksharabhyasam, and Andean Shamanic mountain pilgrimages.

Initiations can look anyway you like. They certainly don't have to be elaborate. Processions, dances, and fire-lit halls may be fun, but a warm, personal letter or telephone call that welcomes a new member can be powerful. A pat on the back with the right words or a dinner with a community gatekeeper can be profound events.

They simply need to be actions that are immediately understood as recognition and welcome. For example, Peace Corps volunteers are sworn in by a State Department diplomat after completing months of training. Each is given a pin with the Peace Corps logo. Employees at the New Belgium Brewery are made company shareholders on their one-year anniversary. They then give a speech to all shareholders explaining what it means to them to be an owner. First-time Burning Man festival goers are instructed to get out of their vehicle and roll in the desert dust three times and then strike a gong on their first crossing into the Burning Man site.

An initiation is a kind of ritual, and the best rituals come with symbols and tokens. Developing a ritual that's right for your formal or informal community can make a profound difference in how welcomed a new member feels. If a clear initiation into the inner ring is missing, then two things become unnecessarily difficult. Newcomers won't know how or when they can become members because there's no clear path to follow.

First, even with a simple initiation, it's clear to all that individuals remain explorers until they choose to cross the boundary. This can set visitors at ease because they know that they're participating without any requirement to adopt the values and beliefs of members if they're not ready to take that step. Second, it's difficult for all participants to understand clearly who's on the inside (and who isn't). There may be a general sense of who the core members are, but less active or new members may wonder about their own status. They may wonder what privileges they have and feel anxious about exactly what constitutes insider status.

Accidental initiations can take the place of intentional initiation. Especially in informal communities, most people look for confirmation that they're accepted and valued inside the community. They'll look for something to interpret as an initiation if one isn't offered. This may be an extemporaneous compliment from a leader, an invitation to teach other insiders, or more intimate invitations away from outer ring activities, such as a private party, an intimate conversation, or an unadvertised gathering. Eventually members will consider some activity a default initiation—even if it wasn't meant to be.

For example, in a formal community like higher education, when college applicants get letters from universities announcing their admission, the message is more than just a bit of positive news: it's an initiation. It's a welcome into an inner ring. It's a moment many people remember for their entire lives. That letter, phone call, or e-mail message acknowledges a boundary crossing. Students know that they're accepted and valued. Opening the letter or answering the call can be a ritual. Universities also offer a welcome convocation so there's a staged ritual for those who not only have been admitted but have accepted that welcome.

Then there's the informal community. I have a friend whom I'll call Scott, who's very well known. He was successful in the music scene early in his career and now lives in an elegant Manhattan townhouse. Many people claim to be his friend, brag that they know him, and angle for invitations to the exclusive events hosted in his home. When he and I first met, we seemed to hit it off quickly and talked about deep and important ideas, but I could see that there were lots of people who were trying to be part of his "inner circle." Many people are invited to his home each week. I didn't know if our relationship would be any deeper than that of the dozens who stood around with glasses of wine and laughed at his jokes.

One day Scott called me late at night because he had broken up with his girlfriend. While we were three time zones apart, he shared his most vulnerable fears with me. I stayed on the phone for at least two hours listening and discussing what his next steps might be. With that phone call, I knew that we really were in an authentic inner ring of friendship together. It was my own initiation to his inner ring. Imagine if, instead, one night Scott had put his arm around me and said, "I appreciate you are one of my closest friends. I know you're not trying to break into show business. I know you aren't asking me to invest in a company and I know you're always honest with me even when we disagree. You're different from 90 percent of the people who visit me. It means a lot. Thank you." That would have been an initiation, too.

The Crisis of Belonging

There's a common phenomenon in many groups, particularly highly selective elite ones, where many members become convinced that they don't belong. This can be true even when each member has been invited inside an exclusive community. When we experience this, we may worry that our own admission was an accident, and, further, that at any moment, someone may recognize this and reject us as frauds.

The tragedy is that even when many members feel this concern, we continue our lives as if this fear doesn't exist. Our community becomes a crowd of individuals, each one lonely and convinced that he or she doesn't belong in the crowd. This is a crisis of belonging.

In the preface I shared with you my discovery that this crisis was rampant among my peers at Yale. I can't count all the hours and words expended by us all to earn our spots in those classrooms, yet many of us feared that someday someone would stop us in the hall and ask us to leave. They would in that moment reveal us as the frauds we felt confident that we were. Fortunately, there's an easy way to overcome this fear. When we feel trapped by a crisis of belonging or notice that others are in this crisis, the solution is simple: extend invitations. *Invitations resolve the crisis of belonging* and as a solution they are so simple as to be almost unbelievable.

The invitations can be to social gatherings, insider events, or one-on-one time. When we as leaders extend invitations, two things happen that break down a crisis of belonging.

First, when we extend invitations, *we establish ourselves as having the power to invite,* no matter what formal role or title, if any, we might have. To those who are feeling a crisis of belonging, getting an invitation from anyone indicates that the inviter is firmly planted in the group and therefore has the power to invite others. This may sound silly, but it's actually how the world works. So when we ourselves feel a crisis of belonging, inviting others to connect with us allows us to plant ourselves more firmly within the community. An invitation to lunch, a walk in a park, or a hot coffee can make a huge difference. We often make invitations more challenging than they need to be. We fear that others will either reject us or simply dismiss our authority.

Second, when those who are trapped in a crisis of belonging receive an invitation from any insider or community leader, *the invitation itself becomes evidence of their belonging.* Their concerns that somehow they were "really" outsiders passing as insiders are challenged; our invitation provides the necessary evidence that they are indeed insiders.

This evidence is so strong that *it's not even important whether they accept our invitations.* Simply providing invitations can resolve their crisis. In the preface I also shared the story of learning how my friend Melo's life was changed by the simple dinner invitations I extended to him. Melo joined us only a few times over three years. No matter: each invitation I extended demonstrated that I had the power to invite and that the others belonged. The genuine invitations, not only the meals themselves, made a difference. The story reminds me that I never fully know the power of my invitations, even those that don't get responses. I simply make them because they can, and do, change lives.

Four

The Rituals Principle

A ritual is any practice that marks a time or event as special or important. The actions are imbued with meaning. They connect the present with things in the past and our hope for the future. The psychologist Roy Baumeister conducted a four-hundred-person survey to distinguish happiness and meaningfulness. His research indicates that "meaningfulness" involves understanding our own lives beyond the present time and place. It comes when we reflect on what came before and how we're connected to the future. Meaningfulness comes when we integrate now with the future and past. Our health, wealth, and relationships change. Meaning creates a feeling of stability in the midst of change. Rituals are a tool to bring meaning into our lives.[1]

Anyone who's spent time in and among religious traditions has noticed that there are rituals for virtually every stage of life, times of happiness, sorrow, and hope. Marriages, death, and even dancing are all ritualized. One of my favorites is the Turkish Sufi whirling dance. It's performed at a kind of sacred concert to attain a trance state. In a totally different way, I admire the Quaker (Society of Friends) meetings, which start silent and can remain entirely so, as all present make themselves open to the divine.

Strong communities create both formal and informal rituals. There are as many types of ritual as your imagination can conjure up. They often rely on special symbols and are important emotionally. Remember: feeling connected, trusted, appreciated, and welcome is all in the realm of emotion.

I believe that because we live in a far more casual time than previous generations, the rituals we keep are even more special now because we don't turn to the institutional rituals of previous generations. In our American lives, blowing out birthday candles, roasting a turkey for Thanksgiving, and sending flowers and cards on Mother's Day are all rituals with which we are so familiar that we may not even recognize them as such. One way to recognize a ritual is to ask whether removing the activity would make the time feel less important. Think about how you and your friends and family celebrate birthdays. What activities indicate that birthdays are more important than other days? What activities make these days "special" for you?

Rituals often have forms (patterns) that participants recognize. We learn these forms after participating in them when the time is right. For example, for birthdays in the United States, we expect a ritual birthday party form that looks something like this:

Friends and family are invited to one place and told there will be a birthday celebration.

Someone prepares or purchases a cake for the celebration.

Someone lights candles on the cake that in some way represents the years lived.

After a meal and unstructured social time, guests sing for the birthday girl or boy.

The birthday girl or boy blows out the candles as fast as she or he can.

There's cheering from guests.

Cake and ice cream are served.

Presents are opened.

Hugs are shared with the birthday girl or boy.

A weekly, monthly, or annual dinner with friends can be a ritual if the gathering becomes special to you. You may even have a friends' gathering that you never thought of as a ritual, but it's a special, even sacred, time for you. You'll get excited in anticipation, you'll arrange your schedule to be available, and you'll arrive prepared in whatever way is important.

My guess is that there are already rituals in your life that you haven't even noticed. It happens all the time. Simple repetition can grow them unnoticed (although repetition does not necessarily a ritual make). For example, a monthly dinner may not start out as a ritual, but after five months in a row, when a friend says that she can't come next time, you may be more disappointed than you had expected—because you've created a ritual without realizing it. It's grown into something more than simply sharing a meal with a friend.

Or your grandmother makes a green Jell-O salad for Thanksgiving dinner for years (and years and years, if she's like mine). One year she makes something else inspired by a *New York Times* recipe, and the guests get upset. Not because the new recipe is worse than the Jell-O, but because the ritual has changed. There was a familiarity and meaning in sharing that family green Jell-O once a year. Simple, unexpected, and unnamed shifts in ritual are the cause of many nasty fights over the holidays. Rituals can mean far more to us than we ever recognize explicitly.

Ritual intensity (how much it affects us) can be increased if we want to. Strengthening a ritual can make it (the activity) feel even more special and important. It's important to do this only with activities that are meaningful to you. For example, imagine if on birthdays in your family, the candle-blowing element was changed so that it included everyone in the family bringing a candle, lighting it in order of birth, and sharing out loud one thing they appreciated about having you in the family for the last year. Then you share what you appreciate about each family member before blowing out all the candles. Wouldn't your birthday celebration feel different, more special? Wouldn't different values have been inserted into the ritual?

There are many ways to make even a simple ritual, like giving a lapel pin, feel more special. For example,

Begin with silence first.
Say aloud why all have come together.
Use a special place.
Touch one another (hand on back, hold hands, hug, etc.).
Transfer the pin.
Say aloud what is now changed.

Ritual silence can be very powerful. Simply keeping silence together can be a powerful part or a whole ritual. It can mean that the relationship is so close that not everything needs to be said aloud and not every moment needs to be entertaining. In a world where every second is filled with talk, music, or alerts, creating the space for silence can be the most powerful time together possible. In my experience, almost every community appreciates a silence ritual when there's painful loss. When I was a chaplain in a trauma center and attended to families in the worst hours of their lives, I saw how important it was for them to have someone sit with them in silence, and even someone who would protect the silence, so they didn't feel the need to say anything. Silence together can be the most powerful time.

Rites of passage are important (and not common enough). They're the most common ritual to notice in communities. This rite is where the community acknowledges someone is passing from one status to another. This can be from one age to another (a birthday), from student to alumnus (graduation), or from follower to leader (promotion or inauguration). The initiation to membership is a rite of passage from outsider to insider. In this rite, the community acknowledges the maturation and growth of a member.

Celebrations often are connected with these rites. The importance of rites of passage and similar celebrations cannot be overstated. They help us feel proud, worthy, and complete as we make important transitions. Whether we're receiving recognition ourselves or offering recognition to someone else in such rituals, we feel valued and connected. My friend Rose-Anne told me how meaningful it was for her when her employer created a ceremony to acknowledge employees who had stayed with the company for certain milestones. She told me that the company gathered employees together and gave gifts according to years committed. To this day she cherishes the candlesticks given to her in that ritual honoring her five years of service. She also felt awe for the recipient honored that day for thirty-five years of service.

These rites are so important that some conflate the ritual (which is a recognition) with the actual maturation or achievement of a person. For example, in President Barack Obama's first inaugural oath, some words were incorrectly quoted. The law was clear that he was nevertheless officially president. But enough people were concerned with the ritual formalities that the swearing in was performed again in the Oval Office to satisfy any lingering concerns. It's important to respect the power that others place in rituals. It's a power just waiting for us to use as we bring people together.

Community display rituals reveal the community to itself. There must be collective displays of participation and community membership. This means that there should be some activities where members can see other members participating as well. The scale and the strength of the community will at least partially be revealed here. These rituals can include anything from formal dress ceremonies to cooperative community service, organized competitions, or anything that displays collective participation. A community where everyone participates individually and invisibly will lack a deeper cohesion.

Play rituals are very important. Communities must have an opportunity to play together. My favorite play ritual is eating together. When meals are ritualized, they become a feast. Virtually every community feasts together in some way. In the United States, Thanksgiving has become the most important feasting ritual for many families and friends. Hosting the feast has become a rite of passage for many young family members and new Americans.

Playing sports and singing are also common. I visited a Hash House Harriers runners group in Chicago. Hash runners are part of an international group that plays a type of runners' game. This includes a pack of runners following a trail laid out earlier by a member who includes dead ends, doublebacks, and misdirection. The runners emphasize socializing far more than fitness. After the Saturday run, we sat next to a lake to enjoy barbecue. While we were all relaxing, some of the Hash members unexpectedly broke into raunchy comedic songs. In the best way, they were demonstrating a community ritual of play and, of course, their insider knowledge. They had a lot of fun, and I felt privileged to be their guest.

A Foundational Ritual Form

It doesn't occur to many people to create new rituals that aren't already part of the group's traditions. But even if a ritual is not yet steeped in tradition, it can still be deeply meaningful. In fact, it could be *more* meaningful because it reflects your time. For every ritual you appreciate, there was someone who originated it and then people who developed it over time. You can be part of the tradition of creating ritual. So how can you create ritual for your community that matters?

I have created many rituals over the years and am still often surprised by how important and powerful they are, both for my friends and for me. They can be minutes long between two friends (like kneeling to ask someone to marry you) or weeks long among thousands of visitors (the Olympics). They can include singing, talking, bowing, or just silence. I've learned from ritual study to include some fundamental elements to make the experience feel deeper and more fulfilling. I call this the "foundational form." It can be used for multiday events (like many weddings) or even a fifteen-minute initiation ritual. It's not important how long each element is, only that each part is truly meaningful to you and your community. I offer the form here as an inspiration only: please create rituals that work for you and make you feel complete and connected.

Foundational Form Elements:

Opening
1. Welcome
2. Intention
3. Reference a tradition
4. Explain events and instructions

Body
  1. Share wisdom
  2. Invite participation

Closing
  1. Acknowledgment
  2. Sending

Opening

Welcome. The welcome marks or "punctuates" the beginning of the ritual time as distinct from the gathering time, or unritualized time. It lets the people who have come together know that the next activities are special (sacred). It's sometimes called the "collect" because it collects the people. Such a collect can begin a meal or a sporting event. In the welcome, all who are gathered are called to focus their attention on one person. That person offers a special welcome to all who have come. This can include acknowledging how far they traveled, what they have given up, and how their presence is important.

> Welcome to our first dinner for international fellows and families series. I acknowledge and thank you for driving here, trusting your friends who told you that this is worth the time, and choosing to spend your evening with us instead of so many options available on a warm night. This is only fun because you join us, share your company, and participate fully. Thank you so much for making this possible.

> Welcome to James's birthday party. I know that some of you took off work, rearranged your schedules, drove over an hour, and hauled children and gear here to join us. It means so much that you've done this. Without you, this is simply a room with food and cake. You make this special. You are special. Thank you.

Welcome to the Oakland games. We have athletes here who have trained for over a year, sought out sponsors, and committed much of their own money to participate this week. We have family members here who have flown thousands of miles to support, accompany, and cheer you. And we have volunteers here who have committed hundreds of hours to ensure that this is a special and important time. I thank all of you for making this happen and sharing this time and your work. You are all welcome in this community as we begin this week's adventure.

State the Intention. The intention of the gathering is stated explicitly. This can be a single intention or several.

We are here to award degrees to our newest graduates, who have completed all the coursework and requirements of the university. We honor you today so that you know you're forever a part of this institution and ambassadors for it wherever you go.

We are gathered for our annual Alejandro family Thanksgiving feast. We're here to celebrate the holiday, give thanks for our abundance, and share time together. Our friendships are by far the most important part of the evening: we're here to share ourselves and strengthen our friendships far more than anything else today.

The world's best winter athletes are gathering in the Olympic Villages. With the Olympic Games we want to show the host country and the world that such a peaceful society is possible, that competition among people can happen in harmony and with respect for the dignity of all. Nelson Mandela said it quite simply: "Sport can change the world." And, indeed, we contribute to a better society. We contribute to peace. We want to prove that respect for rules, respect for your competitors, and respectful dialog can transcend all differences.[2]

Reference a Tradition. This is the time to let everyone know that the activity at hand stands in a tradition or is at least informed by one. This reminds us that we're part of a community that came before us and will likely carry on after us. If neither of those things is true, then you can state that you're beginning a new tradition. You can always say what person, philosophy, or experience inspired the activity at hand.

James and Rena are marrying here as the fourth generation in James's family to marry in Honolulu since his great-grandfather immigrated to this island. Rena is the fourth in her family to create her own family in the United States since she and her family emigrated from Cambodia.

Tonight's dinner comes in the fourth year of this series. It started three and a half years ago here in Brooklyn. Dozens of people have volunteered. Hundreds have participated. The series was inspired by the wisdom of the English writer and theologian C. S. Lewis, who in the 1940s warned of the allure of the inner ring, our own desire to be in a group cooler than our own. He said one way to escape this is to regularly invite others to do something we like to do and create friendship. This is what we continue to do tonight.

In just a few moments, the Olympic Games will officially return to London for the third time. Thank you, London, for welcoming the world to this vibrant city yet again. For the first time in Olympic history, all the participating teams will have female athletes. This is a major boost for gender equality. In a sense, the Olympic Games are coming home tonight. This great, sports-loving country is widely recognized as the birthplace of modern sport. It was here that the concepts of sportsmanship and fair play were first codified into clear rules and regulations.[3]

Explain Events and Instructions. This is where participants learn what will happen in the ritual. It doesn't matter if the allotted time for the ritual is fifteen minutes, two hours, or a week. The explanation orients participants who may be unfamiliar, confused, or even frightened. They will feel more at ease and may even get excited when they learn that you have a plan. If there are rules, then this is the appropriate time to share them (for example, there will be silence, no electronic devices may be used, or newest members sit first). If your ritual has only one "event" (such as placing a pin on a shirt), then you can explain this. If you would like an element to remain a surprise, one option is to tell participants that there will be a surprise. They may appreciate the anticipation.

I'll explain how tonight's Thanksgiving feast will go. I'll explain the menu so those of you with diet restrictions know what's appropriate for you.

When I'm done, Anne will lead a prayer. The buffet will then be open. Grandchildren will go first, making a plate for their grandparents and taking it to them at their tables. Then please help yourselves.

In the other room, you'll each find a seat with your name on a card. At your tables you're encouraged to listen to what's abundant in the lives of the guests around you. This is only a suggestion.

After the main course, you're encouraged to help put away leftovers and wash serving dishes.

When this is complete, we'll serve the pie, ice cream, and coffee. When dessert is served, James and Bill will lead a musical jam session down the hall. All are welcome to join or listen.

After dessert, all are encouraged to help clean the kitchen.

You may stay as long as you like. We'll have plenty of room on the floor!

For this evening's birthday blessing, we'll have a reading from Thomas Merton and other historical religious social activists.

Then letters will be read from friends who could not be here. Stephanie will read the first, and then we'll go around the circle so each person reads a letter until all are read.

We'll then have a seed planting to remind us that our actions grow after we've walked away and in ways we cannot always predict. Each of you is welcome to plant seeds at that time.

Finally, we'll all gather around Naomi and lay a hand on her. If you cannot reach her, then touch someone in front of you. The leader will lead the prayer.

There will then be something we're keeping a surprise.

After, we'll all go in the other room to share our celebratory meal together.

Tonight's event will transition the training week's focus to your work ahead. All participants will remain silent in your seats.

I'll read a passage from Daniel Berrigan about commitment to change. Then, keeping our own silence, Laura will call out your names.

When you hear your name, approach her. She'll give you an envelope that contains a gift just for you.

You'll keep silence and take your gift out onto the property at least one hundred yards from this building. You'll find a private quiet place, and only then should you open your gift.

You will not speak to other participants or interrupt their privacy until at least 10 p.m. At that time, this event will be officially concluded.

If someone wishes to keep his or her privacy later, please honor this preference.

We now have five minutes open for questions, and then we'll begin.

Body

Share Wisdom. Read aloud, quote from memory, or summarize wisdom from anyone important to your community or this event. This can be one simple line or much more. The reference tells participants that the community values wisdom that enriches our lives and is doing something more than making up silly things to do. The examples below are very short. You can use something more substantial. Including wisdom that's more nuanced, poetic, and familiar to you can be far better than my examples.

I remember the wisdom of Thomas Merton, who wrote, "In the end, it is the reality of personal relationships that saves everything." You are my friends, my most important relationships. You save me from everything. I am so grateful.

This is a difficult time. In times like these, I remember the words of the activist priest Daniel Berrigan: "Know where you stand, and stand there." Today we stand here together. You have my respect and honor.

As we begin, I remember the wisdom of Bill Golderer, who created a radical feeding program in Philadelphia: "Be brave in your invitations." I'm so proud to be brave here with you as we do this together.

Invite Participation. Rituals are *much* more fun when all are invited to participate (instead of simply watching). I like to make sure that everyone is invited to do something. This is in contrast to pressuring someone to participate. Sometimes it's a rich experience simply to be present while others participate more actively. Those who choose to participate less actively may simply prefer a more contemplative participation. You can invite participants to do any activity that works for the space and intention. This is the part that many rituals leave out and that makes them boring.

Ideally the activity connects and adds to the ritual's symbolism. This means that there should be *meaning* to the activity, and the meaning should not be too literal. The activity will exist as a symbol and require interpretation. It's perfectly okay if different participants are invited to do different things. For example, participants might be asked to

Present something
Share words or something crafted
Plant a seed
Wash something
Pass something around
Read something aloud
Hang something up for display
Reveal something in the space
Write something
Draw something
Decorate something
Offer a gesture to others, including a hug, bow, or hand touching a shoulder

Closing

Acknowledgment. The acknowledgment states what's complete or changed after the ritual. This gives a sense of accomplishment (no matter how humble) for the ritual. The acknowledgment can be as brief as one sentence or much longer.

> I now pronounce you husband and wife.
>
> Welcome. You're now our newest member.
>
> Again, we've spent time building friendships, and the evening has made at least my life richer and, I hope, yours as well.

Sending. The sending is a way to mark the close of the ritual. In words that are either metaphoric or literal, a leader "sends" participants out into the world to continue life. The sending provides an emotional end to the ritual and gives all a kind of permission and punctuation to reenter nonsacred space and time. It connects us to the future.

> Patricia, you're now a full member. You're a part of our community that builds friendships that change lives, lifts us up when we are weak, and celebrates with us when we are strong. To celebrate this time, let us all leave this place and share drinks in the next room as friends.

> Our Thanksgiving feast is coming to a close. You may all stay longer, even overnight if you prefer. I also know that some of us need to get on the road soon. Thank you for making this year again a special day for all of us, a reminder that we have friends and family who care about us. Please take leftovers with you, drive safely, and let us know how your year goes before next November. Happy Thanksgiving.

This week has been deeply moving. I've made new friends whom I hope to have forever. I've learned a lot about leadership and vision. I've been inspired by what I learned that you're creating. In fact, I can't wait to start helping right away. I hope this is true for all of you as well. We created this week to strengthen leaders who are enriching the world. It looks like we've done this. Now that it's the end, please go back to your homes and your communities and help them to be as inspired with their vision as you are now. The world desperately needs more inspired people. We thank you for being part of this.

Rituals Change

As your community grows through time, it's almost certain that you'll discover that you have rituals (or boundaries or symbols or stories) in place that no longer serve the community as well as they could or should. Communities are dynamic, and so should be the ways you use the seven principles.

The best way to handle this is to reflect on what you want your rituals to mean in this time to the people you include now. You can use elements from the past to keep in touch with your history and tradition and then replace and add elements that excite you. It becomes an artistic and, I hope, fun balance.

Remember the Thanksgiving example, where people might want routine. While you'll be upset if Grandma's green Jell-O isn't on the Thanksgiving table, you'd probably also be upset if the Thanksgiving meal were *exactly* the same as it had been in 1949. The guests have changed, and likely the location as well. Perhaps in addition to the turkey there are now vegetarian entrées and a more diverse menu. New guests have brought in dishes from their own traditions.

Is it meaningful to include food traditions that come from your guests' families? Is it a good idea to change timing to support families with babies and long drives? Can the table be set differently to accommodate someone in a wheelchair? Only you can know based on the kinds of values (like belonging) you want to incorporate. If you're stuck keeping your traditions exactly the same, then know that you're likely maintaining something that will grow less meaningful and appropriate for a community that won't remain exactly the same.

A dynamic community needs dynamic growth in its rituals. All symbols and rituals serve their purpose for a time. They shape people, communities, even nations. And time moves on. The history and meaning behind a ritual and symbol is revealed and understood with new perspective and sensibilities. People will ask whether should we hold to our tradition or should we release the past and adopt new symbols?

Consensus is never easy in these times. Seeking consensus is useful, perhaps necessary. But the process, no matter how well intentioned, rarely offers a better solution. Whether we choose one position, its opposite, or some middle ground, there will always be some left upset. In the end, good leadership will realize that the ultimate responsibility cannot be dispersed to the larger community. This is one of many leadership moments that requires a brief consultation with an inner compass. A decision to create the future instead of simply towing the past must be made.

Five

The Temple Principle

We all want a place where our community gathers and we can do things that we long for in our everyday lives. A temple is simply a place where people with shared values enact their community's rituals. Members know that it's where they'll find their community. Members who are far away may long to visit. In some ways, the temple represents the community's strength and legitimacy. It's a "sacred space," a place set aside for a particular use. A designated permanent temple is nice, but not necessary: any space can be made a temple simply by members gathering there and enacting rituals. In fact, a clear field is certainly a temple for some sporting communities.

No matter where I travel, no matter in what city, there's always a place set aside for a faith tradition nearby. This tells me how much we want to gather in a special way no matter where we find ourselves in the world. One of the most moving sacred sites I have ever visited is the Sikh Golden Temple in Amritsar, India. Sacred texts are read aloud, people pray in a manner consistent with the Sikh tradition, and every person who visits is welcome to a fresh hot meal at any hour of every day. There's no restriction for religion, class, or background. Over thirty thousand visitors every day are fed as much as they like for free. Afterward, all are invited to hot chai tea outside. All is prepared, served, and cleaned by volunteers in a giant "Langar" (free kitchen) on the temple grounds. I've learned from friends that this hospitality is continued around the world where strangers are fed at local Sikh Gurdwaras, although on a much smaller scale.

I've also visited a fairly secret sacred Native American site on the California coast. The space there is designated by little more than wood huts and a cleared space. The managing medicine man doesn't share with outsiders what rituals go on there. I do know that every day Native Americans from far away seek out this place.

The rituals performed inside a temple might be considered weird if performed outside and seen by outsiders with no explanation. Within the temple, they're meaningful and comfortable. Insider knowledge allows the rituals to be experienced as satisfying and even fun. Here are a few examples of rituals that would look weird if they were done outside the understood time and place set aside for them:

> Hoisting a shirt with a big number on the back high into the air (at a jersey retirement ceremony).

> Soldiers with guns standing completely motionless in perfectly clean uniforms next to a parking lot (greeting a hearse in Arlington Cemetery).

> Middle-aged people walking in a line wearing black robes and then reciting in Latin (at a university graduation).

Some people feel free to sing, dance, and express themselves emotionally only within rituals. These could include weddings, sports events, or holiday festivities.

Creating Sacred Spaces for Your Community

A sacred space is simply a space set aside for special purposes. When you think about spaces that are special for you, you'll probably think about something that happens in that space that doesn't happen elsewhere. Also, some activities are more special if you do them in a particular place. Weddings are a good example. You can get married pretty much anywhere, but most people want to get married in a place they consider special.

The space has profound impact on any ritual experience. For example, imagine a wedding in a bathroom at Penn Station. No matter what the happy couple wears or who officiates, the ritual will feel grimy. Now imagine the same ceremony inside the National Cathedral or in Central Park's Sheep Meadow in New York City. If you're like me, the same ritual will feel meaningfully different and more important.

The environment in which an event occurs affects the tenor of the ritual and the emotions of the participants. Similarly, even a pat on the back and a hug from a parent at the Pantheon in Rome may feel profound because the space helps make it so. When you consider rituals for your community, it'll make a difference in the impact of the ritual if you choose a space that's meaningful to your community.

You can make a place a sacred space momentarily. Any space can be temporarily set aside (made sacred). All you need is to designate it as sacred when you use it for something special. For example, a backyard may be used for lots of activities, including grilling, sports, and sprinkler dancing. It can be made sacred anytime by a preparation that's meaningful to you. This may mean gathering particular people in it, inviting particular words to be shared, or decorating it in a special way. There are several features you can use to easily create a sacred space. Anything that works for you is appropriate, and you don't need to use all of them all the time. Below is a list to help you think of ways to create temporary sacred spaces.

Boundary. Something indicates the space boundary. Just as membership boundaries help make a community, spatial boundaries help make a place sacred. The edge of a clearing, a line of flowers, a room's walls, or anything else can serve to mark the special inside of the sacred space. Even laying a rope around a space can help.

Invitation. People important to the ritual are specifically invited into the space. Their very presence makes the space sacred.

Clothing. Participants wear special clothes to the space when it's sacred. This can mean dressing up or wearing something deemed appropriate for the occasion (robes, uniforms, special hats, etc.).

Lighting. The lighting is shaped for the ritual. It's best if light is thrown where attention is wanted and minimized elsewhere. Placing candles is one way to pool light where you want it.

Sound. The sound is different when the space is sacred. If a space is usually loud, silence is special. If it's usually cacophonous, then melodiousness is special. Sound, as much as visuals, will change the feeling in the space.

Height. Objects important for the ceremony are raised up, including people. This can include someone during a ceremony moving from floor level to a raised level. Or simply standing up. If it's a dinner ritual, for example, the leader can stand up to make a toast or welcome. It makes that space more sacred.

Any leader can create a temple for members to gather. We choose what and when to designate a place as a temple. Chances are, an informal temple will naturally emerge if one isn't formally designated. You can identify temples because members make a pilgrimage (travel) there because it's meaningful to them and the place represents their values and community. The more secret and inaccessible the temple is to outsiders, the more satisfying it feels to enter, though concealment limits growth and access for visitors and explorers.

In the CrossFit community, the World CrossFit Games competition in California is a type of temple. CrossFitters gather there to compete, celebrate, and share their own stories with one another. Many CrossFit athletes aspire to both attend and compete in the world games. To traditional competitive athletes who carry a ball or speed over long distances, the CrossFit games are definitely weird. CrossFitters strip nearly naked, do Olympic weightlifting, and then walk on their hands, flip tires, and more. They even often cheer loudest for the athlete who's last to finish! To insiders, this is simply a reflection of their values.

A large community will almost certainly create minor temples. A community can have many temples of varying importance. In other words, a single temple is not the be-all and end-all. A minor temple is simply a place where members gather and enact rituals that either is smaller than the primary temple or is used by a subcommunity. These minor temples allow smaller groups to know one another more intimately, have their own style of rituals, and even differentiate themselves from the bigger, maybe global, community.

For example, CrossFitters have world games each year that serve as a kind of temporary global temple. In addition, for each member, the local gym is a minor temple. Members gather there regularly and perform a heavily ritualized workout. In a typical

CrossFit gym, workouts last one hour and include dynamic warmup, skills training, strength training, and metabolic conditioning.

I've visited CrossFit gyms from Connecticut to Texas and California, and I can recognize the ritual in each place, even though it's interpreted differently. Some training is repeated more often in different locations, and, goodness knows, the music changes. Outsiders may find some parts of the ritual weird, such as the frequent fist bumping, weight dropping, and collapsing to the floor. Visiting CrossFitters, on the other hand, feel welcome when they find all this no matter how far they are from home. They get to visit the intimate special place (minor temple) of distant members in the same greater community.

I share this distinction because you may have a community that's too big or too spread apart to have one sacred place. Think about what small spaces you could make special and how similar (or different) you'd like them to be from one another. Just as the urban dweller CrossFitters in Mexico City train differently from the beach CrossFitters on Oahu, you may prefer to make each minor temple different, and just right, for its own intimate group.

I learned that Twitch's members enjoyed meeting one another at live video game events so much that they have created meet-up groups in many cities so they could continue to connect offline. In other words, members have created their own minor temples so they could find their community even when Twitch wasn't inviting them to a large live event.

Using the definition in this book, an online destination can absolutely become a type of community temple, though obviously with meaningful differences from the places we gather offline. The temple is created as soon as members know that they'll find their community there and they can enact some rituals meaningful for them. You probably already know that there are many online destinations where members find people who share their values. Later, in Part 3, "Advanced Ideas," I discuss some ways online communities apply the principles in specific ways.

A well-built and well-managed online community can be great, but even at its best, it still doesn't provide the same high level of connection and feeling of belonging as meeting offline can. I discussed this with Stu McLaren, who founded WishList, which powers over 42,000 online membership sites. He also coaches many companies on building online communities. Even he believes that *the most powerful thing an online community can do is create offline friendships.* He encourages every community to create at least one annual offline event that members can join. He also understands the power of inviting individuals to a temple where they can meet their community and share stories, learn from one another, and celebrate successes.

Six

The Stories Principle

Stories are the most powerful way we humans learn. Every community, like every person, is full of stories. Sharing certain stories deepens a community's connections. If people don't know (or can't learn) your stories, they don't know or understand your community. They can't know who you are, what you do, or how what you do matters. Stories are how members, future members, and outsiders learn the values and the value of the community. The stories must be shared so that members can understand the community's authentic values and identity.

Anyone familiar with a religious tradition knows at least a few iconic stories that are core to the tradition's identity. Canonical and sacred texts including the Muslim Qur'an, Christian Bible, Jewish Torah, and Buddhist sutras are full of stories. Some are historical and others metaphoric.

In all great religions, there are stories that must be known if one is to understand the tradition, such as the Buddha's enlightenment under the Bodhi Tree, the Israelites' exodus from Egypt, and the Mormon story of Joseph Smith's revelation by angels and golden tablets.

Origin Stories

Among the most important stories are origin stories. By definition, these stories explain how something started, i.e., its origin. There can be different origin stories for different parts of a community. But there must be a *single* origin story about how the founders were inspired to form the community. The story must include how they learned something new, did something new, and then invited others to join them.

Ideally, community origin stories are true—but what "true" means can vary. There are many ways to tell any story by selecting what's shared and what's left out. Origin stories are often considered true if they share factual, emotional, or ideological truth. They are strongest if all three are represented.

Community origin stories communicate who the community serves, why it serves, and often how it serves. More important, stories also share values. Stories do this far more effectively than a mission or values statement ever can. As communities change over time, the origin story will expand or new origin stories will emerge to explain how the current community differs from earlier versions. The new stories will all share how the community faced new challenges and responded accordingly.

For example, thirteen years ago, the Lowell Mothers Community (not its real name) started when twelve new mothers met in a breastfeeding group hosted in a local church. They were excited to meet and created supportive relationships outside the original group. Out of convenience, they set up an online community to support one another with babysitting, carpooling, sharing nannies, and good mothering advice. Other mothers joined the online community, and the larger membership brought more resources to serve one another. Now, over ten years later, thousands of mothers connect, seek help, and support one another, including many who live far beyond Lowell.

Sharing Values Stories

There must also be stories about how the community's values are expressed and how they affect real people. These stories will tell everyone far more about the community identity than everything else combined. When you think of communities you appreciate, consider what stories are told to newcomers and shared over and over again among members. These stories represent the values all hope to embody.

Katie works for New Belgium Brewing. Founded in Fort Collins, Colorado, in 1991, this beer brewing company prides itself on a collaborative culture, making employees owners and keeping the company financials open for all employees to see. Katie shared with me a story that's really important for her about her company.

Early on, its leadership wanted to find a way to use low- or zero-carbon emission energy to power its operations instead of coal-sourced electricity. There was an opportunity to do this, but it required the company to sign a contract for ten years of wind power and pay a significant cash advance. As the story goes, the company had the money in hand but had already promised it as year-end bonuses for the employees. A meeting was called, and the company founders explained the situation, then left the room. After an hour of discussion, all the employees agreed to skip their bonuses so that the company could run on wind energy. The story tells Katie that she works in a community that will make hard choices and take actions consistent with the company's environmentalist values. Its leaders would even incur costs to maintain the integrity between what they say they value and what they do.

Sharing Vulnerable Stories

As Brené Brown now famously discusses in her book *Daring Greatly: How the Courage to Be Vulnerable Transforms the Way We Live, Love, Parent, and Lead*, vulnerability is when we share something we fear may cause others to reject us. This includes uncertainty, risk, and emotional exposure.[1] Strong communities share stories in which leadership, members, or even the overall organization was vulnerable. These stories build strong bonds. They may include accounts of failure, or the fears, feelings, and truths we don't want the whole world to know. These stories are so important that if they're not shared, and the vulnerability and intimacy is never built, there will almost certainly be a superficial feeling of connection among members and with leadership.

For example, Marcus, the director of programming at Twitch, was in charge of community there when the company was already serving tens of millions of users a month. A few years ago, while Twitch was upgrading its back-end software, the company accidentally deleted days of video archives for the "Twitch Play Pokemon" (TPP) phenomenon. TPP invited Twitch users to play Pokemon using Twitch chat. Over *one million* users participated.

Marcus explained that by any standard, the archive loss was a big failure. When the mistake was discovered, there were several options for how to handle it. Marcus was proud to tell me that instead of hiding the problem and hoping to resolve the failure secretly, the company stood by its value of transparency. Marcus personally contacted the leaders of the TPP community with over 150,000 users. He admitted that the archives had been deleted and told them that the company had assigned four engineers to retrieve the videos, although no one knew how or when they'd fix the loss. It took weeks. Marcus strongly believes that the honesty in admitting failure in this example and others built lasting trust with Twitch users.

Sharing Personal Stories

Members need opportunities to share their own stories, whether in formal or informal venues (or both). This helps them feel that they're seen and understood. It also helps members understand the shared values in the community. These stories share the real challenges people faced and how those challenges shaped the teller's current character.

Consider the communities to which you feel most connected. My guess is that there were opportunities, even informal gatherings, where you got to learn and share personal stories. These stories may be the most important part of your experience. They can include how members recovered from sickness, overcame grief, or simply got through a tough project. It's possible that sharing your stories is a way to make an investment in a particular community. This can radically change a community if the stories are dear to you. The community can feel more like "your" community because you've entrusted it with a piece of yourself.

My friend Emily works for a famous movie studio I'll call Neptune Studios. She recently told me about a time when one of the company's middle managers (not an executive) learned that her daughter had been diagnosed with a neurological disease that meant over her life she would gradually lose function and eventually not be able to care for herself. While there's no cure, there's ongoing research to find a cure, or at least therapies that can help.

Filmmakers at the studio wanted to help. Many artists at the studio make world-famous characters and stories, and they came together and created an art auction of personal work, putting several hundred pieces up for charity auction at Neptune. After hearing about the auction, company management agreed to cater it. The event raised significant funds to reach a cure or treatment for the sick child. This story tells Emily that the Neptune community cares about more than making movies and pocketing profits. She works at a place where people care for one another and will create the extraordinary to help. It makes her more comfortable and committed every day.

If you are a part of a community that is dear to you now, you may not have noticed that learning stories like these that are in the community made you feel more deeply connected and welcome. Maybe you have noticed. In any case, as we invite others to join us in our most important communities, giving them a chance to learn and share the most important stories can make a world of difference. This can even happen over coffee, across from a campfire, or walking up a mountain. How are your members learning and sharing stories?

Seven

The Symbols Principle

Symbols are powerful tools in building community because they quickly remind us of our values, identity, and commitment in a community. Using symbols is a way to make communities stronger. Symbols represent a set of ideas and values, which is to say, they often represent many things at once. They can conveniently stand in for many words.

Anything can be a symbol. This includes the flame symbolism in the Unitarian Universalist tradition and the purifying water in Hindu tradition. In consciousness traditions like Taoism and Buddhism, symbols tend to be more abstract. For example, the yin and yang represent in part how things that may appear opposite are in fact complementary. In theistic traditions, such as Christianity and Sikhism, the symbols are often taken from iconic stories. The Christian cross comes from the story of Jesus's crucifixion. The Sikh crossed swords refer to a turn away from pacifism to defense of the vulnerable. In any tradition, there will be many symbols for different times and places. Simply changing a robe color or donning a head covering can symbolize a special time.

A community symbol is far more than a pictorial representation of a single word, idea, or memory. In fact, community symbols work best when they're *not* too literal. Literal symbols leave less interpretive room to represent numerous and evolving ideas. For example, the circular Peace Corps logo is a symbol for the worldwide Peace Corps community, both current and past. It includes a dove within an American flag. As far as I know, there are no actual doves on American flags in Peace Corps service. Note that the symbol doesn't include a depiction of an American digging a well or teaching in a classroom. If it did, the added literalism would weaken the symbol's power.

Or consider the official Marine Corps emblem, which depicts an eagle sitting atop a globe with an anchor through it. Obviously it's nonliteral. It's also a symbol tattooed on the arms of many Marines. If you were to ask many Peace Corps volunteers or Marines what their symbol means to them, you would get somewhat different answers from each group. But no matter the diversity of answers, in both cases the symbols represent their communities and a set of values.

Communities often use many symbols. In fact, this is almost inevitable. Some symbols will naturally emerge. Others can be thoughtout and chosen. Symbols usually reference a story, place, or tool that's important to the community's history. What's most important is that you recognize the power of symbols and how much members appreciate them. They can be potent tools to remind all who you are, what you do, and why you matter. Ask yourself, what are the symbols your community uses? If you have none, what elements should your community's symbol include?

Tokens as Symbols

A token is a kind of symbol given to a person as a keepsake to remember an idea, event, or set of values. It's often a reminder of accomplishment, belonging, and commitment. People love tokens. They often have powerful meaning when leaders or peers present them in rituals.

You likely have tokens (formal or informal) from your own community experiences. Sometimes we get our own tokens: souvenirs are a kind of self-gotten token. But tokens are much more meaningful when others give them to us. The importance of the token's presenter will imprint on the token's value. For example, if Nelson Mandela were to give me a single South African rand as a token of thanks, that coin would be more meaningful to me than dozens of more obviously valuable thank-you gifts.

After I completed my Peace Corps training in Zambia, a State Department officer officially swore us in at a ceremony in front of our instructors and the Peace Corps country staff. During the ceremony, he fastened a Peace Corps logo pin on our lapels. This ceremony was a rite of passage recognizing our journey from trainees to Peace Corps volunteers. The space was made sacred by inviting special people into it and asking us to dress nicely (at least by Peace Corps standards!).

Each pin became a token for us to keep as a reminder of our initiation, accomplishments, commitments, and belonging in the community. They weren't expensive: any one of us could have purchased one hundred pins before the ceremony. But the pins we were *given* became special.

My friend Joel is a search and rescue dog handler. He tells me that when a team makes a real difference for some military or government group, a "challenge coin" from that group is presented as a gift. The coins are custom-made for the group and typically include the unit's insignia. They obviously have little or no exchange value. But they mean a lot to the recipients because they're given with intention and meaning. They represent appreciation and respect.

In mythical stories of heroes growing to maturation and power, useful tokens are often items given by wise elders to help the hero on his or her journey. The token's value is not apparent when it's received. During the journey, its value to help or even save the hero is revealed. Symbolic tokens in our own lives can serve a similar purpose. They can represent wisdom, support, or teachings generously given to us by elders or peers to help us on our journeys. They remain as reminders that others are rooting for us and want to be supportive in our lives.

The only limit to the number and types of tokens is your imagination. But at some point, just as with all things, if there are too many, they lose their value. If there are too few, then they don't offer the power that they can. You'll have to choose when and what you can offer as tokens to help others remember their belonging, accomplishments, and commitments. Anything can be a token. Pins, scarves, medals, flags, and certificates are commonly used. Even a small rock can make a perfectly good token if presented in a sacred way. The tokens for your community should represent your values.

Many tokens remain unseen until we identify them. Tokens are like rituals in that they can be created and appreciated without becoming identified. Items that start out simply as useful and practical can in time become infused with meaning. For example, when my grandmother could no longer host Thanksgiving gatherings, she passed on the special platters and serving dishes to my father and mother. These became tokens that represented hosting, family, connection, welcome, and some authority, even though they started as items that presented food. Leaders can notice everyday objects that can be imbued with powerful meaning, and those items can be passed on as tokens. It can be a simple matter of replacing the item with a new one to let the old live on as a symbol. A pen used for signing, a glass used to toast, or a hat worn on a special adventure can all be passed on and replaced.

Tokens can be very powerful when we give them to others. Remember that the giver can imbue value into the token. If this is done honestly and intentionally, the token's material value may not matter at all. To use the power of tokens we can use a few simple principles.

Intention: Tell the receiver why you're giving it to her.

Symbolism: Tell her what it represents to you.

Connect to the future: Tell her how you hope it will support, change, or serve her.

Stephanie, I'm giving you these candleholders. We've used them for over one hundred dinners here. At least a thousand people have gathered around these at some point, making friendships. I'm giving them to you because I know that you'll use them. I know that you bring people together in a welcoming space and invite them to share themselves. These holders represent hospitality, creating a prepared space for others to gather. I hope that they make your space more cheerful and remind you that your efforts are important even if you don't see the results.

Eight

The Inner Rings Principle

We all want to be special to someone or several someones. We all want to be valued and valuable. This could look like joining the elite club of Academy Award winners, Olympic athletes, or Nobel Prize winners. There are formal inner rings with official membership, and there are many more informal inner rings. We all aspire to belong to prestigious inner rings, perhaps not just for authority and respect but for new ways to participate and contribute. This desire is so powerful that we're rarely satisfied with the rings we already inhabit. We simply differ on the inner rings we aspire to join and what we're willing to do for admission.

I've not yet discovered a single spiritual tradition without some sort of inner-ring organization. The most beautiful description I've heard was by my friend and Tibetan Buddhist teacher Lama Surya Das. He explained that in his tradition these rings can be mapped on a mandala, a circular figure or diagram that represents wholeness and the universe with material and nonmaterial parts. As one travels deeper into the community, it can be described as a journey from the outer part to the inner part and then to the secret or subtler part. The journey from the periphery into the inner rings can be described in this way:[1]

Interested Seekers
Students
Joining Members
Practitioners
Lay Vowed
Acolyte or Neophyte Vowed
Monastic Vowed
Mystics and Sages

The progression may look like a hierarchy, but it's not. Every part of the mandala is the center, and every part is connected to every other part. The heart center, or the mandala's center, "is bigger than the space outside." In other words, for those who enter the smallest inner ring, they'll find that in the center there is oneness where all are linked. New members are concerned about what they can get out of the tradition. The mystics and sages in the center are concerned for all beings in the universe.

Almost everyone aspires to join inner rings (if you are normal). When I lived in New York City as a young documentary filmmaker, I aspired to join an inner ring of professional documentary filmmakers. It was an informal ring that socialized at particular locations in the city, meeting up at filmmaking events including certain workshops, festivals, and panels. But when I succeeded in joining this group, I realized that the ring I *really* wanted to join was the ring of PBS filmmakers, then a ring of filmmakers whose work was funded by a particular list of funders, then a ring of international award-winning filmmakers, then a ring of filmmakers whose work was distributed internationally on television and via other media, then the ring of filmmakers who won an Academy Award.

The members of each progressive ring, I believed, could teach me more, have better wisdom, have access to more power, better understand how to accomplish goals, and maybe even have more

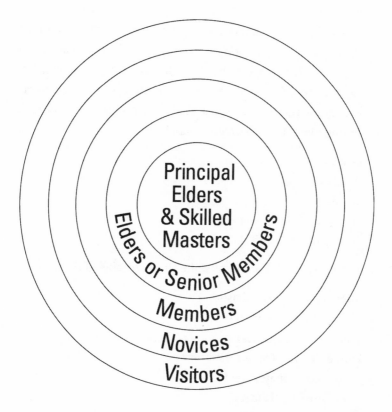

fun. Obviously this was not always true. These were informal rings. There were no group presidents, selection committees, membership cards, or annual meetings. I wanted to continue into these inner rings all the same. For better or worse, I saw the progression as a reflection of my own growth, even as important for my continued advancement. I wanted evidence that I was becoming a more established filmmaker. Inclusion in these informal inner rings was one way to evaluate my success at the time.

The endless striving for the next ring can be a dangerous trap. In mature and formal communities, there's a much more satisfying and healthy way to relate to inner rings. Mature and strong communities create different levels of inner rings that members can enter (not to be superior snobs but to serve differently). At each level, members gain some benefits related to their maturation or formation. The benefits could include new access, knowledge, authority, acknowledgment, or respect. Groups have many different names for these inner rings. A typical progression will look something like this, with different labels:

Visitors
Novices
Members
Elders or senior members
Principal elders and skilled masters

In our dinner series community, the rings are labeled this way:

Information seekers (visitors)
Dinner guests (novices)
Volunteers (members)
Dinner leaders (senior members)
Leader coordinators (elders)
Hosts (principal elders)

A community can decide what makes an appropriate inner ring and how many there should be. Obviously there's a point at which it becomes pointless and silly: imagine an organization with only ten members and seven inner rings! Even small organizations, however, will see at least a few informal rings form.

It's *not* important that each member pursue inner rings. Not all members in our dinner series aspired to be a dinner leader. It's perfectly fine for a member to find a preferred level and remain there. Success in life or in the community should never be defined only by progression into increasingly exclusive rings.

Strong communities offer a journey (progression) into successive inner rings. While some members may *choose* to stay at a particular level, mature communities provide *opportunities* to progress in their series of inner rings. In the best examples, the progression reflects a journey of growth or maturation.

This is true even if the community is based on a shared interest or skill like bicycling, gaming, or dinner parties. One type of growth can simply be a level of skill or competitive achievement (for example, bicycle racing, kite making, or boat building). Evaluating improving skill is one way to evaluate the journey across levels. But skill improvement (e.g., making higher-flying kites) is a superficial measure that may usefully organize a group, but not a community.

The most powerful journey reflects "maturation" of growing concern for others. On this journey, we follow a path of progression during which concern for ourselves diminishes while concern for the others—an ever-widening circle beyond ourselves—grows. The irony is that the smaller and the more exclusive the ring to which we belong, the broader our concern for others.

Visitor: May have concern for no one else, seeks novelty or fun experiences.

Novice: Concern for individual self, seeks personal achievement and legitimacy.

Member: Concern for one's peer group, seeks success and respect for the group.

Elder: Concern for everyone in the tribe everywhere, seeks the whole tribe's success and respect.

Principal elder: Concern for the whole world, seeks to help the worldwide tribe fit within and serve the dynamic world.

Not all communities have principal elders with a whole-world perspective for their tribe, but the most respected communities often do. Again, consider our dinner community as an example with this idea in mind. The descriptions below articulate the minimum maturation required within each level. If individuals never achieve a level's *minimum*, either they won't advance or they'll make very poor advanced members. This example highlights how skills alone are not enough to make the next inner ring appropriate for someone's journey.

> Information seekers (visitors): Not concerned yet for anyone else, seeking knowledge about the series.
>
> Dinner guests (novices): Concerned for self to have a good experience.
>
> Volunteers (members): Concerned that guests have a good experience and perhaps learn skills themselves.
>
> Dinner leaders (senior members): Concerned that volunteers and guests have a valuable experience.
>
> Leader coordinators (elders): Concerned that all the leaders, their teams, and guests create something valuable and fun.
>
> Hosts (principal elders): Concerned that all involved get value and the series enriches the community it lives within and makes a difference in the future.

The 1984 film *The Karate Kid* presents a good example of how crossing inner rings is a journey into maturation. The film tells the story of a boy named Daniel who's seeking a karate master with whom to study. Daniel starts out as a visitor to the karate tradition: he wants to learn to defend himself. The gatekeeper who can teach the martial art controls the entry into the inner ring of the tradition. Daniel learns about two apparent skilled masters, the calm Kesuke Miyagi and the violent and aggressive John Kreese. After Daniel's pleading, Miyagi agrees to teach him. The training assignments are strange and seemingly pointless: Miyagi instructs

Daniel to do menial tasks all day, such as painting, sanding, and washing. Only after Daniel completes several days of boring and painful assignments is the wisdom behind the training revealed. Daniel, a novice, is encouraged to *do the behavior before understanding and believing in their value or philosophy.*

Then the training philosophy is revealed and after he has developed karate muscle memory through the tasks, Daniel becomes an insider. Miyagi gives him a headband as a token of his new status. When Daniel completes his training, Miyagi gives him a competition uniform with a bonsai tree depicted on the back. It's a token of Daniel's transition from student to competitor given by his senior elder. He'll take it with him through the upcoming challenges.

In the third act, Daniel enters a karate competition. He's asked what color belt rank he has. This question is designed to determine if he's really an elder-level insider. Miyagi, a skilled master, assures the tournament official that Daniel is a black belt (elder). He can approve Daniel's authenticity as a gatekeeper in the karate community. Though other competitors have much more experience, Daniel reaches the final match. Throughout, he is the only competitor wearing a Japanese rising sun headband, the token from his training.

In the semifinal, when it appears that Daniel could win, Kreese instructs his competing students to "show no mercy" and to hurt Daniel. They do. Then, even with a hurt leg, Daniel wins the championship match with a flying crane kick. He's lifted up by the crowd and recognized by all as a mature elder. We see that he's grown and can now defend himself and presumably others from threats that, before his journey, would have overwhelmed him.

The most interesting part is how the two karate instructors are presented. We can tell that Miyagi is the real principal elder because Kreese is interested only in the welfare, success, and recognition of his own group; he's clearly *not* concerned with the welfare of strangers. This is revealed in the first act when he refuses to ask his students to respect Daniel. Nor does he care for the karate tribe in general. We know this because he tells his students to hurt Daniel in competition. We see that Kreese is really an immature member pretending to be a principal. He has skills but not the maturity that makes a true principal elder.

Miyagi, on the other hand, defends Daniel when he's a stranger and cares for all karate competitors. This is made explicit in the sequel film when Miyagi protects one of Kreese's students from Kreese's own abuse. Both we, the audience, and the karate competitors can see that Miyagi is an authentic elder not only because of his skill but also because of his broad concern, even generosity. We also have a sense that Daniel has found the right path to follow. If Daniel continues to study with Miyagi, he will also mature into a true principal with far more internal growth than just physical growth.

Even a principal elder never achieves "all" knowledge. Miyagi may say that he has learned from Daniel as Daniel has learned from him; Kreese, of course, wouldn't admit that a student could teach him anything. So a true principal can learn from novices, members, and others as much as others learn from her. What the principal learns will be very different from what the novices learn, and how the novices teach will be very different from how the principal teach.

In creating inner ring journeys, we offer opportunities to teach. As we progress into ever more exclusive inner rings, we want new ways to express both our own and our community's values. This could consist of additional opportunities to practice an activity, develop a tradition, or teach others. But because the best inner-ring journeys teach us to care for increasingly wider circles of people, advanced inner rings must give members an opportunity to teach others—to share not just skills but values and beliefs that help us mature internally as people. On our journey, we want to be taught, and we also want to teach. This is why creating opportunities to both mentor and be mentored are powerful.

For a healthy and growing community, it must be clear how one crosses into inner rings. The journey may be difficult, whether naturally or by design. This difficulty is what keeps the inner rings exclusive. But the path must be both known and available for those who are willing to commit and learn. For example, in our dinner community advancement required a commitment to scheduling time, planning a meal, recruiting volunteers, funding an evening, and hosting an event for four hours. When a volunteer could do this, then that volunteer would become a fully recognized dinner leader.

Whatever the path is, it should help foster the member's maturity and include an evaluation that assesses this maturity. If you choose, this can mean informal teaching by more senior members or a formal evaluation from leaders. Some new members will have skills and maturity that are more advanced than that of their peers. Those members should cross into inner rings more quickly, in a way that reflects their journey. As long as each ring's values are honored, members should be allowed to progress at their own pace. If all members are forced to progress at the exact same pace, then *time* is honored more than *maturation*. This is an unattractive and uninspiring path. For the right reasons, talented and skilled members will get frustrated and likely leave. This can be particularly important in a corporate setting. Talented people want to know how they can progress in the company or their own field. If it's unclear how they can do this in your organization, then they'll look for options elsewhere.

A Dangerous Inner Ring Trap

As I mentioned in the preface, C. S. Lewis explained the attraction and danger of pursuing an inner ring in his 1944 speech, "The Inner Ring." The trap of the inner ring is the spiraling cycle that pulls us from one ring to the next; as soon as we achieve one, we inevitably long for the next, even more exclusive (and thus more attractive) ring beyond it.

> The desire to be inside the invisible line illustrates this rule. As long as you are governed by that desire you will never get what you want. You are trying to peel an onion: if you succeed there will be nothing left. Until you conquer the fear of being an outsider, an outsider you will remain.[2]

For example, admission into an elite school is an invitation to join an inner ring. But when we arrive at the school, we discover that there's a group of cool kids who have formed a better, and more exclusive, inner ring. If we enter that ring, we discover yet another, more exclusive ring of student organization leaders, presidential scholars, or sports stars. Beyond that ring, we discover a still more exclusive ring of accomplished students. There we discover that there's an inner ring of society presidents and alumni, and so on: the inner rings go on forever. Even if we become president of our own country, we'll discover that there's a smaller inner ring of world leaders who have won the Nobel Peace Prize. Because an even more inner ring will always exist, our aspirations can never be satisfied. Without awareness and conscious effort on our part, we will fall into the self-created trap of striving to be somewhere that we are not.

My friend Patricia shared with me that when she entered law school, she heard how prestigious it was to work on the law review. In fact, the current US president served on the same publication! It sounded so special that she immediately wanted to join that exclusive group. Then, over the next weeks, she considered what she wanted to learn in law school and what she wanted to do after law school. She wanted to work on international justice. The hours on the law review wouldn't really help her do that as much as other opportunities. It wasn't a good investment of her time except that it might result in becoming an elite insider. She told me how hard it was to let go of the draw of the law review inner ring and return to pursuing what inspires her.

Lewis says that there's nothing wrong with inner rings in and of themselves. They're simply structures filled with people longing to be connected. What he warns us against is our insatiable desire to pursue new rings. Once we recognize this desire, we can choose to give it up.

There is a way to escape the inner ring trap. Lewis recommends that we participate in some activity that we enjoy and do it often. His example is playing music. We can then invite others who would like to join us in playing music. As we regularly gather to do this, we'll form a specific kind of relationship that saves us from longing to be elsewhere. That relationship is friendship. This is the real foundation for a community. Remember our definition of community? A community is a group of individuals who share mutual concern for each other's welfare. When we form a community that grows friendship, we *create* what we seek, friends who care about the welfare of one another. To outsiders, it may look like an exclusive inner ring. We'll know, however, that it's open to anyone who shares our values, even if this is simply valuing friends with whom we play music.

Saving Us from the Inner Ring Trap

Avoiding the inner ring trap is why our communities must offer clear paths to personal growth for those who share our values.

This access prevents us from creating meaningless inner rings that remain unattainable (and pointless). If we *consciously* create inner rings with our communities, and build them based on our core values, and invite anyone with those same values to enter, we create a forum for friendship. For example, when we started our dinner series, we sent out invitations by e-mail across the campus and beyond. Anyone was welcome to join us as long as they reserved an available seat early enough. Within the first four months, it became clear who our regulars were. They helped set up, and they knew where our supplies were kept. They helped with the flow of the long evening. Eventually some regulars began leading dinners. We called them dinner leaders. A few years in, the series grew so large that our friend Arjan began coordinating and Sam handled administration.

Graduate and undergraduate students, faculty members, administrators, visiting lecturers, theologians, medical doctors, journalists, human rights activists, ethicists, poets, and rocket scientists joined us. I learned how rare it was for students to sit down for three or more hours, connecting with others, uninterrupted and without an agenda. For many, the dinners became a highlight of their university experience. A funny thing happened in the second year: two regulars, Courtney and Bjorn, told me that when strangers discovered that they had been to "the dinners on Prospect Street," the strangers wanted to know how to get invited, how to get inside what of course looked like our inner ring. Several of us laughed about this. We knew that we had worked hard to create a system for *anyone* to join, as long as they RSVP'd on our public website! We learned that this simple commitment to share dinner created something that indeed looked like an exclusive inner ring to others. What we really had was a community of friends always ready to welcome more. If you want to learn more about our dinner series community, I share more as an example in Appendix B.

The Diaconate

A community may have many different inner rings. Some may lead naturally into other rings. For example, airline pilots may have a more exclusive ring of airline captains. Within that ring, there may be another for airline captains who fly international routes. Other inner rings may not have any more exclusive rings. For example, my wife is in a community of Cambodian women professionals in Oakland. There's really only one ring among those particular women. But an increase in the group's size might inspire or require, down the road, the creation of more inner rings. Most mature communities have at least one ring, if not a hierarchy of rings, that I call the diaconate.[3] Like *temple* and *rituals*, the term *diaconate* comes from spiritual communities, but can be applied to all kinds of communities.

The diaconate are people who have more authority in the community than other members. The diaconate should also have more wisdom about the community, but that's a best-case scenario. Their opinions are more valued than those of other members. The diaconate is always made up of members who are elders and leaders. The gatekeepers mentioned earlier are part of the diaconate. They obviously have more authority. In this age, it's likely that your members will respect the diaconate and maintain its legitimacy because members believe that the leaders are or could be their friends. Members believe this because they understand that the diaconate embodies the community values that members hold dear.

Such authority can be either helpful or abusive. We have all seen both. Danger usually arises when leaders no longer prioritize enriching members but think of themselves as infallible and forbid any questioning of their moral rightness. The diaconate has informal or formal authority in three key areas:

Protecting the boundary: They have the authority to exclude or reject someone from the community, ideally for lacking values consistent with the community.

Officiating at rituals: Their attendance makes rituals either important or more important. These can include formal rites of passage like initiations or informal celebratory feasts.

Teaching on community values: Their teachings on community values are more influential than those of other members.

Think about the communities you value. Whether there's a formal structure or not, there are almost certainly people who have more authority than others in these three areas. There may be a single person who has responsibility for all three domains.

There are ways to identify the diaconate in a community. In an informal community, there may be no titles that would help an outsider identify the diaconate. There may even be pride in *not* appointing an official diaconate. But a mature and strong community always has a diaconate of some kind. Members may simply refer to these people as popular, respected, influential, or a "big deal." You can usually identify the diaconate by answering these questions:

Who has the authority to reject someone from this community?

Who can bring someone into the community on his or her say-so?

Whose attendance makes a simple gathering more important or exciting?

Who are the members to whom the rest of the community will (almost) always listen?

Whose wisdom and insight is repeated within the community?

Whose approval will allow or expedite an idea that can change the community?

Problems arise if there's no diaconate. Some communities pride themselves in giving all members, even visitors perhaps, an equal voice. Part of the idea is to ensure that no one can be left out or drowned out. It's certainly true that good ideas and maturation can come from the least appreciated member. This is often how young communities start. But strict egalitarianism leads to problems as communities grow larger, do more, and mature in philosophy. At some point, ideas aren't all equally valuable. For example, new members who are uninformed about the community history may make suggestions that have already been tried, and have failed, many times.

Without a diaconate, there's no way to differentiate the contribution of an Einstein from that of a village bonehead or crackpot. If both are given equal consideration and time, then the overall community will grow upset. Moreover, visitors will be unable to tell if the community itself can distinguish between an Einstein and a crackpot. Rightfully, they'll question the community values and fall away. A more dangerous possibility is that some members will advocate for values that conflict with those of the community, like violence, racism, or xenophobia. Without a diaconate, it's impossible for the larger community to rightfully tell outsiders that these radicals don't reflect the core community. The diaconate allows boundary enforcement so that radicals can be forced out, perhaps to create their own separate community.

It's important to identify the diaconate, even an informal one, because new and maturing members will want to know what the values are and what's permitted (that is, what allows one to stay in the group). Without a diaconate, visitors won't know what (if any-thing) the community stands for. They won't know if they're listening to the uninformed village drunk or the moral backbone of the community. There's a common cycle in the role of the diaconate, as informal authority moves to formal authority and then schism, which starts the cycle again in a new community. As a community matures, the need for a diaconate grows.

I mentioned my friend Amanda, a member of what I call the Lowell moms community. Over time, other mothers joined the small initial online community, and the larger membership brought more resources to serve one another. As new mothers joined, they were put into smaller cohorts (inner rings) so they could discuss the issues relevant to newborns. The membership has grown to thousands of mothers, including those who live beyond Lowell. The online platform-managing moms and forum managers became the formal diaconate even without an election or any of the current members aware how they got the authority. Amanda loves getting support from and providing support to the mothers in her cohort. She especially looks forward to seeing them offline in parks or visiting one another in their homes.

This past year, the online leaders decided that the community had grown too large and announced that they would end membership for anyone living outside Lowell. As you can imagine, this generated outrage from many members, some because they were getting rejected for their zip code and others because they would lose connection with friends for a seemingly trivial reason.

When Amanda told me about this, it sounded like a classic example where the leadership values something (proximity and management ease) and the membership values something different (participation and support). Amanda explained that the moms in her inner ring handled the tumult by moving their online connection to another social media platform. There, the Lowell moms leaders couldn't impose rules (based on values) that Amanda's ring didn't like. Amanda's ring had its own leadership.

She didn't call this a community schism, but it certainly looked like one to me.

Over time, values will almost invariably shift within a community: becoming more or less inclusive, choosing different priorities, or setting more ambitious goals. A values debate will begin, and a new informal diaconate will rise, advocating the new values. If the formal diaconate does not recognize the importance of the informal one, there will be a schism. This isn't necessarily a bad thing. It can simply mean that subgroups with differing values are differentiating themselves. To prevent a schism, the diaconate must continually accommodate evolving values in the community. At some point, the new values may no longer fit in the original community. In this case, allowing some members to fall away may be the best choice.

Mature Communities Lead Growth

Mature and strong communities give members opportunities to learn how to succeed in some way. That is, they help members grow in a way they would like to grow. The community supports growth and may explicitly lead this growth. This growth can be toward managing life as a whole or in some specific skill set or area of life.

For example, succeeding as a mom, entrepreneur, or bush pilot are all pursuits that communities can help us achieve. Strong communities teach members how to succeed in ways they cannot achieve on their own. The education comes from a body of knowledge and wisdom that members cannot access or manage on their own. So, in a strong community, members must know how to access the knowledge held by others. This can be informal (by hanging out with other members) or formal (with personal lessons, classes, or apprenticeships). If members no longer believe that the community can teach them how to succeed, their commitment will almost certainly fall away. Alternatively, if members have a sense that somehow membership can help them succeed, but they don't understand *how* membership does this or how they can gain access to the wisdom, training, teachers, or mentors, then the community is weakened.

Members want to be taught by (and share time with) community elders. It's important for elders to have opportunities both to teach and to learn. They're resources for skills, internal health, and member-only knowledge. They can do this formally by hosting classes and retreats, or informally through unstructured conversation and private invitations. Imagine how differently visitors would experience that large urban church if elders invited new members to dinner, private walks, or classes on how the church creates its activism. The community would almost certainly have grown stronger.

As a New York filmmaker, I joined several documentary film groups. I went to social events, screenings, and panel presentations. I desperately wanted to grow as a filmmaker and have the wisdom that comes from the experience of being an international documentary filmmaker. I didn't know what I didn't know. But I did know that I could access this only by talking with veterans. You can imagine how disappointed I would have been if I had attended those events and the veterans were separated from the new filmmakers by a red rope, an all-access pass, and a knowing smirk. Fortunately, this is not how it happened. I had fantastic, life-changing conversations with filmmakers in lobbies, over dinner, and in theater lines.

Many of us share fairly universal goals. It's possible that you have a community that just looks like a group of friends, or people who live near one another, or people who are related to each other. You may not think that the community you have or want to build is helping with any particular growth, success, or skill set development. You may be right: I haven't met your group.

Consider that even if you didn't necessarily gather originally to succeed at a skill set, there are some common goals in life that each member brought to your community, and your community is helping with them. Just about everyone wants to achieve some combination of the two goals below. In this context, they're neither good nor bad. They're simply the things that we worry about without even knowing why much of the time. If your community can help others handle one or more of these, it's doing a great service indeed.

The first goal is to belong, to be welcomed somewhere and to connect with others. In 1943 Abraham Maslow wrote about a psychology theory on the hierarchy of needs. It's widely used to understand people's priorities. The theory places "love & belonging" in the middle of the hierarchy.[4] In other words, after shelter, food, and safety, we need love and belonging, which are even more essential than esteem and self-actualization.

The psychologists Roy Baumeister and Mark Leary write: "The belongingness hypothesis is that human beings have a pervasive drive to form and maintain at least a minimum quantity of lasting, positive, and significant interpersonal relationships." In other words, deep connections matter. Baumeister and Leary are not the first psychologists to say that belongingness is important, but they provide a nuance: that belongingness is created through "frequent interactions, plus persistent caring."[5]

It may be that we want to belong so much that we'll conform to a group simply to not stand out. As early as 1951 the research psychologist Solomon Asch put subjects in a group that conspired to misstate which drawn line appeared to match other lines in a set of three. Three out of four subjects conformed to the group and agreed to what they knew was wrong.[6] Our longing to belong may be so strong that we'll deny what we believe to be true.

The fear many of us felt in middle school when we knew we didn't fit in and wondered if we ever would, never completely goes away for most of us. It may be built into our nature. I've gotten better at remembering that there are friends and family who support and cheer on my success. Despite that, the panic of not being good enough, of never being fully welcomed, of maybe being left out or seen as a fraud, still haunts me sometimes. Every day I want to know I fit in somewhere and I belong.

The second goal is to contribute to someone or something. Even in the early stage of psychology, one of the founding minds of the field, Alfred Adler, postulated that "the only individuals who can really meet and master the problems of life . . . are those who show in their striving a tendency to enrich everyone else."[7] It's not just that many of us want to contribute. Contributing actually helps make us healthy and feel better.

Social research by Carolyn Schwartz in the past fifteen years indicates that "both helping others and receiving help were significant predictors of mental health . . . [and] giving help was a more important predictor of better reported mental health than receiving help."[8] A study by William Harbaugh at the University of Oregon put subjects in an fMRI machine while they decided how to split money between themselves and a local food bank. The research indicated that giving money away to charity activates the same pleasure centers of the brain that are also activated with exposure to cocaine, art, and attractive faces.[9] Last, a survey by Baumeister and colleagues found that being a giver was positively related to experiencing meaningfulness, while being a taker diminished it.[10]

Over the years, I've spoken to thousands of people on five continents. Some are almost mythically successful and internationally famous. Some don't have access to enough food. Wealth and geography don't make a difference in wanting to make a difference. If

your community helps members make a bigger or better difference, then it's of tremendous value. This alone can be the bind-
ing value of many communities. The Byron Fellowship is a great
example of a community formed explicitly to support members'
growth. For over ten years, the fellowship has brought together
about twenty-five social change leaders from around the world
and from widely varying fields for a weeklong workshop. In this
experience, they learn to clarify their intentions, visions for the
world, and their next steps during a secluded training intensive.
After the week, fellows and "mentors" (instructors) participate in
the ongoing fellowship community through self-organized events
and projects, and by staying connected through an online community. Some fellows go on to volunteer in future trainings, and some
return to lead parts of the weeklong workshop themselves.

The fellows go on to support one another as they create programs, develop their strategies, and take on fund-raising goals.
The fellowship was founded by Mark Boyce and Gabriel Grant,
who met at Indiana University, where they worked to grow education on sustainability far beyond the current offerings. They discovered a mutual passion for creating a living laboratory education experience. If and when the community no longer helps these
members grow, make a difference, or know they fit in someplace,
the membership will dissipate.

On one notable occasion, the Byron Fellowship failed painfully
at enriching fellows as intended. The directors changed the schedule to involve more mentors. In the process, the plan's bigger goals
were never effectively shared with the mentors. The conversation
in planning meetings and session evaluations revolved around
keeping the schedule moving. As you can imagine, the programming was exhausting for all involved. The days felt like a race.

On the fifth day, the new fellows called an unscheduled community conversation where they expressed their own dissatisfac-

tion. They (rightly) felt rushed. They didn't feel confident that they had enough time to wrestle with the ideas presented or spend time building the relationships they longed for with one another. In short, they staged a strike and refused to continue with the schedule as planned. The good news is that the directors responded to these concerns, and the remaining days were rescheduled with the whole community in conversation. The event also prompted a deep reflection on what the program was trying to create during the week and an attempt to find what was obviously missing to achieve this.

I mention this experience because it's a great example of leadership intending to provide more value to members but, in the end, doing the opposite. Gabriel did bring the fellows together, brought in instructors, prepared presentations, and scheduled field trips, but he actually failed to help them grow in the way they wanted to that week. If the program didn't find its way in growing members, then its future would be in doubt. In this case Gabriel learned that more time was needed for reflection and relatedness among fellows. He changed the programming for the next cohort. This participation breakdown hasn't happened again.

External and Internal Growth

Communities offer external and internal growth. Almost all communities teach members some external skills. These can be as varied as hitchhiking across Africa, hosting dinner parties in America, or creating a more supportive neighborhood. The strongest communities also teach their members how to improve internal health, including emotional and mental growth that cannot be learned from books or videos.

My friend Alison is active in a meditation community in San Francisco. She began attending the evening sessions to learn how to meditate, including posture, breathing cadence, and scheduling practice time. She learned how to concentrate on her breath, to visualize her body full of white light, and to create healing meditations. The more she participated, the more her skills grew. But far more important was her personal growth—she began noticing her own desires and personal pride. The more she noticed these, the calmer and more content she felt. This gave her a new way to relate and connect to people. Such internal growth couldn't be learned from a book. No one in the group is really impressed if she can now sit for hours at a time. Her internal changes, even if for moments, are the marker of true growth.

My friend Bjorn was a Boy Scout for many years. He learned a "ton" of technical skills, like tying knots, building fires, and treating wounds. Officially, he advanced based on his technical skills, for which he received merit badges. But Bjorn sees now that the true growth was learning to live out his values. He understands that the real value was supporting him to grow into a person who seeks to help others and remains physically strong, mentally awake, and morally committed. It's no surprise to him that these are tenets delineated in the actual Boy Scout oath.

That real growth could never have been learned from Scout manuals. It grew over time, in relationship with Scout mentors and peers on a similar journey. In communities that you value, you may recognize skills you learned that anyone could get from a book or from much practice. I hope that you also recognize how communities have come to shape your character and maturity. That's the value that makes a community so much richer than a collection of how-to manuals or a series of classes. Communities provide the time and space for that internal growth to happen among friends.

Strong communities teach esoteric knowledge. In mature communities, there are at least two kinds of "insider knowledge" that are only intended for or only truly understood by insiders. The first kind I call "data." This is information that's shared only with people who are determined to have the right intentions, integrity, and values. For example, I know of a professional women's business group that shares salary information with other members so they can all understand how women are paid in their field. This is meant to help rising professional women negotiate appropriate pay when the time comes. I also know that my search and rescue friend Joel knows codes, meeting locations, and security protocols shared only with credentialed responders.

There's also a more powerful kind of insider knowledge that indicates belonging. I call it "perception." Perception comes when members learn either from explicit teaching or from experience that certain things are not as they appear to outsiders. Access to this esoteric perception is one of the jewels of membership (formal or informal). Remember *The Karate Kid*: karate for self-defense looked like fancy moves, aggression, and arrogance, but Daniel learned that true karate includes growth in humility, determination, discipline, and respect for the tradition and the elder who teaches it. Earlier, I explained how rituals may seem silly to outsiders but meaningful to insiders. It's the esoteric knowledge that allows insiders to appreciate what outsiders cannot understand.

For example, my friend Alison participates in Weight Watchers. She knows that losing weight is not *simply* about eating less, as general outsiders may believe. Weight Watchers members know that achieving and maintaining a healthy weight includes working toward understanding and accepting self-worth, personal identity, feelings, expectations, and daily discipline. There are levels of emotional and mental health that must be addressed for long-term success.

Then there's my friend Patricia, who's part of a storytelling group in her city. The members know that the most powerful storytelling is vulnerable and creates strong and treasured connections. Storytellers need a private, safe, and respectful space to offer their full selves in order to move and inspire listeners. Outsiders think storytelling is about entertainment and deft wordcraft. They cannot understand why members would share vulnerable stories with people they don't know.

My search and rescue dog handler friend Joel has told me that outsiders think his work is fun and exciting. Insiders know that how they and their dogs perform and the choices they make are critical for someone's life when the calls come. There's a lot of complication in considering how someone behaves when lost and in finding relevant information. Those searching feel enormous responsibility. The work is filled with seriousness and long, cold hours.

I'm hopeful you understand how important and sophisticated inner rings can be for a growing community. It is easy to make a meaningless ring series for member glorification. It is far more rewarding and rich to create rings that serve and help members grow. Who doesn't want to share time with people who help us become who we aspire to be?

Part Three

Advanced Ideas

Nine

Distinguishing Religion and Avoiding Cult

The principles in this book have been used in spiritual and religious traditions for millennia. I'm confident that you've recognized how these principles show up in the spiritual organizations you know. I assume that you aspire to build something that's *not* a cult and probably not your own religion. While it's true that both religious traditions and harmful cults use many of the principles I've outlined above, you can dip into the wisdom of religious tradition and still build something very different. While almost all dogs have tails, putting a tail on something doesn't make it a dog.

Common Features of Major Religions

Specifically defining what is and is not a religion is challenging by itself. There are communities in which their identity as a religious group is debatable. For example, while Buddhism is considered one of the five major religions of the world and included in university religious studies departments, I have spoken with Buddhist monks who do not consider their tradition to be a religion. Nonetheless, religions typically have specific ways of including the following four features within a broad range of agreement.

First, they have an origin myth for the universe. The faith tradition has a literal or poetic story about how the universe is created. This story informs the nature of moral rightness and the meaning (or lack thereof) of our lives. Religious origin myths are *very often* not interpreted literally. Such myths are considered poetic. By this I mean that the story imparts a moral truth through themes and metaphors. This can be the case when the true nature of the supernatural is believed to be beyond the understanding of our limited minds and certainly our language. The stories often remind us that we are sourced from something and we are connected to a global community that goes back much farther than our memory. Such a universal origin myth is different from the literal and true story of a community origin. I would expect that your community origin story limits creation to your community and not to that of all beings in the universe.

Second, there's a particular cosmology, broadly speaking. A cosmology is a body of thought, doctrine, or understanding about the natural order of the universe: that the universe was created by God, or is entirely an illusion, or is the manifestation of supernatural forms we cannot access. As with the origin myth, cosmological descriptions are often metaphoric. The cosmology helps us understand our place in the world, even if the understanding is limited and poetic. While members often share a cosmology (and I imagine very seldom discuss it as such), most communities you'll participate in won't advocate a particular cosmology.

Third, there's an agreed source of moral truth. Any given religious tradition agrees on some entity or idea that points to moral truth. An example of this might be how to understand when our own actions are moral or immoral. Even in spiritual communities, such a generally shared understanding of moral truth rarely makes important moral choices easy or clear, but the traditions at least provide a source that members can turn to. This is different from simply agreeing on what relevant choices are moral or immoral. In secular communities, members will share some sense of moral agreement (so members can get along). Rarely will you share a rubric for what makes universal moral rightness. It's perfectly okay to handle what's fair and good for your work and the issues you're dealing with. This may mean agreeing on how to demonstrate respect, honesty, and support. You don't have to agree on what makes moral things moral on behalf of the cosmos.

Fourth, there's a particular epistemology, or way to identify truth. Epistemology is the theory of knowledge—how we know what's true. Everyone has a general way of knowing how to recognize truth. Whatever you understand is true, there's a way that you came to believe this. You may not be aware that you have your own way of deciding what's true. Epistemology is not only for religions. You can believe things are true simply because someone you respect told you (a teacher), or you saw something and your interpretation is all you need. For religions that include belief in a supernatural realm, there are ways that supernatural truth is revealed to us in the material world. How that is revealed is for another book. It's unlikely that your community will create a worldview that instructs members how to fundamentally know what's true.

Common Features of a Harmful Cult

Cults are also difficult to define clearly. The term has meant many things over the past three centuries, and today it's used very differently in religious scholarship and colloquially. The term is often used pejoratively to describe groups others fear or simply don't like. For my purposes here, I'm including features of *harmful* cults that can lead people to do things they previously would have thought horrible and even to harm themselves over months or years. If you avoid the features below, you can confidently avoid creating a cult.

If we remember that the most important thing about a community is serving members to enrich their lives and connect to a dynamic world, then we can see how these features can easily lead members away from this goal.

For clarity, let me explain that simply because group members dress and talk alike, spend a lot of time together, talk about how much they love the community, and invite others to participate doesn't make them a cult. This could describe many high school marching bands or a cooperative grocery store in Brooklyn. A true harmful cult has a far higher (or lower) standard.

Absolute moral authority resides with the leader alone. The leader has unquestioned and irrefutable superior access to moral truth. This means that whatever the leader says is right: followers can have no meaningful discussion about its truth.

Leadership is not accountable to anyone else. The leader is not accountable to any higher authority. This is unlike ministers, monks, and rabbis of mainstream religions, who have higher bodies that can evaluate and restrain them.

Unquestioning commitment to the leader is required. Members must demonstrate unquestioning commitment to the leader's belief system, ideology, and truth. If they fail, they'll be rejected. This is very different from a group that simply agrees on a general ideology or a belief system. This feature is about members being unable to question or reconsider what the leader teaches. Expressions of doubt or dissent are punished.

Isolation from the outside is encouraged. Members are encouraged to cut their ties with their outside community, including family and friends. This isolation is coupled with strong encouragement to socialize or live only with cult members. This is very different from a community whose members simply choose to spend a lot of time together.

Exit barriers are high. The group makes it difficult, and sometimes impossible, to leave. This can be done through physical, emotional, or psychological threats or blackmail, or through financial manipulation. In a healthy community, members can leave whenever they decide that their values are no longer in alignment with those of other group members.

Worldview is polarized. The group has an us-versus-them mentality with the world. This is the opposite of a healthy community that considers itself a part of the dynamic world and seeks to enrich the world with its work and teaching.

Ultimate moral permission rests within the group. The group believes that its exceptional status and its all-important ends justify whatever means members choose to achieve their goals. These include activities members would have considered unethical, reprehensible, or illegal before joining.

Obsession with growing the group is central. The group is focused on acquiring new members rather than on enriching the lives of current members or accomplishing other goals.

If these features are not part of your community and you have no intention of including them, then you're likely building something very different from a cult.

Healthy Features for a Strong Community

When you upend unhealthy features found in cults, what you find is a list of positive features that the best communities possess. Your challenge is to find ways to strengthen these features in your communities.

The leader has bounded moral authority. All members have some understanding about moral authority. Members can question the moral truth in actions or ideas. Respectful discussion on controversial topics is understood as important and necessary. When a leader has gone beyond moral propriety, others can remove him or her, denounce the action, and correct what must be rectified.

Commitment to the leader is limited and contextualized with other commitments in a member's life. A member's commitment to the leader's belief system, ideology, and truth is limited and contextualized within other commitments and values. This can include family, work, and spiritual values and commitments. A group may simply agree on a general ideology or a belief system and also explore questions that confront the belief system or ideology. Dissent is welcome as long as it's respectful and allows the group to function to serve members.

There's engagement with the outside. Members are encouraged to engage, enrich, and participate with the outside community, including outside family and friends. Whatever members get from their insider community will enrich the parts of their lives that happen outside the community as well. If a community spends a lot of time together, there's awareness that family relationships and outside friendships are also important and need attention.

An exit is always available. Members can leave whenever they see that their values are not in alignment with the group. Members know how they can leave. This can include never attending gatherings again. Members are never threatened for leaving, though remaining members may be disappointed and express this respectfully.

There's a connected worldview. The group sees itself as part of the greater dynamic world and seeks to enrich the world with its work and teaching. This can include global service efforts or simply local efforts to create friendship and connection.

Leadership has accountability. The leader is accountable to a higher authority. This may include a formal or informal elders group, funders, or the general membership. This is similar to how ministers, monks, and rabbis of mainstream religions are subject to higher bodies that can evaluate and restrain them when their behavior falls outside the community values.

There's bounded moral permission. The group believes that its status as part of a dynamic world means that it must consider the moral rightness of its actions and goals. The group knows the moral limits applied in the outside world also limit its own insider actions.

Growing the group is a priority equal to others. The group welcomes new members who share its values. This includes discussing values, inviting participation, and sharing how to achieve membership. Growing membership is no more important than serving members and never important enough to lie, trick, or pressure visitors to join. The group believes only visitors who are honestly inspired by the membership and the real values of the community are right for membership.

Ten

Managing Community Face-to-Face and Online

In this chapter I share advanced ideas about managing community that can help as you grow communities over the long term. These ideas focus on three areas. The first is based on understanding that people seek at least three kinds of success and that choosing community leaders who seek the right kind of success is very important. The second looks at how the seven principles can be applied to online communities to enrich them. Lastly, I share an introduction to the work Elinor Ostrom, whose community management insights can help you avoid painful pitfalls.

Different Kinds of Success

Earlier when I discussed progressive inner rings and the kinds of rings that make up the diaconate, I mentioned that it's important that our domain of concern expands as we progress into inner rings and gain more privileges. There's danger in inviting people with a selfish orientation to success into roles of authority. Of course, many of us have priorities beyond pure self-sacrificing generosity. There are at least three ways people seek success: Relative, Personal Maximization, and Community Maximization. In our own lives, we may default to one of these orientations at different times and areas in our lives. How we each seek success at work, in our family, or through philanthropy may look very different.

Achieving Relative Success

When we seek relative success, we simply want to do better than other people—probably better than everyone else. While in principle this isn't a bad idea, in practice it means that we may seek our success by making others win less. We may even gain less for ourselves if our relative success is higher than others. Other people's success becomes a threat even if it doesn't actually erode our own success. Their success may even enhance my own, but it'll look like a threat to me. I'll get upset simply because someone else has (or may have) more success than me. For example, when we're picking apples, I'd be okay hiding apple buckets from you, even though that time is taken from my own apple picking. I'm more interested in collecting more apples than you.

As you can imagine, this orientation means that I'm not very interested in cooperating or being generous unless I learn that I can succeed more than you when I cooperate. Most of us don't want to follow people who relate to us by hiding our apple buckets. Those who seek relative success can be proud of short-term gains, but in the long run this kind of orientation precludes building the strong, intimate, and dependable relationships that matter when things get tough (especially when apple buckets are being hidden). It's also exhausting trying to simply beat everyone else at winning things, especially when no one else really cares.

Achieving Personal Maximizing Success

Personal maximizers simply want to succeed all they can. It doesn't bother them if others also succeed equally or even outperform them in the task. This means that cooperation is welcome as long as it increases my own success. Using the apple-picking example,

Advanced Idea: Remember that the best principal elders are concerned not only about members in the community but about those outside it as well. The limit of our concern should dictate the bounds of our authority. For example, if I'm concerned only with the success and well-being of my own city club, then I shouldn't wield authority over the national organization. When we can consider the whole world to be the community we seek to serve, then we have transcended sectarian selfishness. This is a high bar. For me, I'm pretty happy when I discover I'm not a selfish jerk all the time. One advanced way to think of progress and maturity in advanced inner rings is growing the group for which we're willing to generously seek success. It's perfectly okay for us to also be enriched in the journey.

I'd be happy to work together, splitting responsibilities like picking, ladder moving, and bucket hauling so that at the end of the day my take is increased.

The shadow side of personal maximization is that it's still a fundamentally selfish orientation. As soon as I think that cooperation doesn't specifically benefit me, I'll stop. This means that when things get tough or even unsure, cooperation is fragile. Most of us like to work with someone through hard times, hard conversations, and hard decisions, and know that they'll stick with us to the end.

Achieving Community Maximizing Success

Community maximizing success seeks to do whatever will make us as a group succeed most. In this orientation, we don't necessarily prioritize who within the group wins the most as long as we maximize the total group success. This means that not only is cooperation welcome but I'm willing to reduce my own personal success (sacrifice) so the group wins more. How much I'll sacrifice is up to me. This is a generous way to participate. Whether I actually do erode my own success or not, this commitment is inspiring. When apple picking, I'll shuttle others back and forth from the road if that will help the group the most, even if my personal pick of the apples may not necessarily be maximized.

A community maximizer does not *necessarily* have to reduce her own success or be a martyr. In fact, she may (accurately) notice that in the long run, maximizing community success creates a community that supports and cares for her as an extension of the friendships and connections she's developed. Further, working for community success may actually lead to the best personal success. The important part is that she's willing to participate, even lead, though others may *apparently* win more than she. My guess is that when hard times come (and they always come), she'll have the relationships that hold her up on the worst days, because she has an authentic community of support.

I hope that you can see how the first two kinds of success described above, relative success and personal maximization, are at their core selfish orientations. Others might also win when we pursue those kinds of success, but it comes as a side effect or even as an accident. In this short discussion, only the community success is truly altruistic. I've used the example of apple picking to explain these different orientations. In the real world, success isn't that easy to measure. In communities, we care about access to things, popularity, titles, and whatever perceived cachet there is to gain. I've noticed that at weddings, people even care about where their assigned seat is placed relative to the bride and groom.

We can look carefully at whom we're encouraging or supporting to take leadership and consider what kind of success they're looking for in a community. We don't need to find only the most self-sacrificing leaders who are pure of heart (if we can find them). We can consider what kinds of success our leaders are working for and consider how that pursuit will enrich the whole community. I promise you, when you get relative success seekers in leadership, it becomes no fun for members. Who wants to follow someone who's seeking success at your expense? The heart of community cohesion is threatened.

For those who appear stuck in a selfish success orientation, this section may be hard to understand. In fact, they may not even believe that there are people who actually do things for community success when it may erode their own personal success. They don't believe that we're honest when we share that we want to see others win. They wonder what our ulterior motive is. Anything we do to support others can come back to us in goodwill, a returned favor, or a future invitation. That's just the way the world works.

You yourself have probably done many things in your life where you were pretty sure you wouldn't get a return. If you did it because you care about the welfare of other people, you shared a bit of generosity. One of your jobs as a tribal leader who wants to serve and enrich others is to find and reward leadership that's truly committed to community success. This doesn't mean that true community leaders never gain from their participation. It simply means that you seek the people who care about others and can put at least a part of their own ego and desires aside when they bring people together.

Managing Online Communities

After speaking to several online community leaders and professionals who build or manage growing communities with thousands or millions of members, I was surprised and delighted to learn how much the seven principles of community building also come into play with online communities. Though the principles may be applied differently, nevertheless they're all there. The online community managers I spoke to used a different language for the principles we've covered, but they recognized their importance.

Online Community Relative Strengths

The first strength of an online community is that it can overcome the limitations of geography and time. This means that members can find each other and connect wherever they are. Anytime someone wants support, needs to check in, or looks to learn something new, the Internet is open. No one needs to get to the clubhouse and unlock the doors.

Second, when it's important, members can protect one another's offline identity. While this can reduce the feeling of connection or trust compared with an offline community, this can be a positive feature that allows people to connect and feel safe. For example, those suffering with addiction rarely want colleagues at work, neighbors in the park, or relatives at family gatherings to know what they're dealing with. Maintaining their anonymity is important. Creating a venue that makes it safer to connect can be a welcome resource.

Third, scaling (growing bigger) is fairly easy. Online communities are not restricted by a physical building, parking availability, or venue. It's relatively easy to invite and include new members. Twitter, for instance, allows many people to follow and learn from an individual without taxing the teacher. For the same scale to happen exclusively offline, a great hall would be reserved, sound systems set up, and hours of travel possibly required.

Fourth, the experiences, both with text or video, can be easily recorded and offered to members as resources. The important but casual conversations in an offline meeting or training are much harder to share widely unless they're imported into an online community.

Online Community Relative Weaknesses

While relationships that develop online can be powerful and life enriching in the aggregate, it's difficult, if not impossible, to develop the level of connection and intimacy that's available in offline communities. Whatever else is true about online communities, this is an important consideration when you calculate how much activity you want to encourage online versus offline among your members. Even Twitch, with over one hundred million members and untold terabytes of content, brings members together at offline events in huge arenas.

Virtually all of us want friends for emotional reasons. If we simply wanted technical help, we'd spend much more time with books and instructional videos. Emotional presence is difficult to share online. Who knows if and when that will change? When a parent dies, a partner dumps us, or a frightening diagnosis is received, we don't want a video conference of people to turn to. We mostly want friends and family to join us in the room. We want to feel their hugs. The offline parts really matter. It's also more difficult for visitors to understand how much they belong to an online community. We can't see where warm bodies are congregating. This may mean that gatekeepers may need to be more concerned about helping visitors *feel* welcome and find a way inside the community.

Online Community Identity

Like offline communities, online communities must have a vision for their existence. This includes what values draw members. The vision must be clearly shared by the managers in some way. Make sure your members and visitors know why you created or manage your community.

Along with the vision, members must know how the group supports and leads their growth at least in technical skills and ideally also in internal maturity. Stu McLaren, the WishList founder, says that strong online communities also help with handling fear, self-doubt, and anxiety. These feelings are rarely shared, but a community that puts these issues in the open gives members both permission and a safe place to grow through these challenges. The sharing becomes vulnerable, and this vulnerability creates deeper connections.

Using the Seven Principles for Belonging

Boundary. Members need to commit in some way to join. Often a paywall is an effective boundary because members know that other members paid something to participate. The lowest barrier is sharing your name and e-mail address. This minimum barrier shows that they're committing to enter. Stu also recommends a set of required questions that include why members want to join and what they want to get out of their participation. Once inside, a good manager will make the community a safe space by offering supportive words and useful advice right away. It's also important that managers are not critical of new members. The manager participates in making the space a venue for growing and sharing vulnerable truths.

Initiation. There should be a welcome routine for new members. This routine encourages them to get involved as quickly as possible and build relationships with other members. This can include an announcement to current members and a specific welcome from an elder (including diaconate). Other members can reach out and find commonalities. The routine should help the new member to feel seen, understood, and welcome to participate more. Since we know about the importance of symbols, a badge can be displayed that represents the cohort or particular ring she or he is now a part of.

Rituals. Rituals are more challenging online than offline. However, they're no less important. Celebrating milestones in someone's life is important. I learned of a community of entrepreneurs that announces and celebrates six- and seven-figure sales milestones. Another group celebrates exercise commitments completed (miles walked). Patientslikeme.com provides an online platform for people to share health experiences in order to help themselves, other patients with similar challenges, and organizations that focus on medical conditions. They have over four hundred thousand members who discuss over twenty-five hundred medical conditions. On their site, members with life-changing diseases celebrate difficult daily accomplishments that would go unnoticed by outsiders. This includes getting out of bed or going for a walk. Another online community is Quitnet.com, founded in 1995 to help people quit smoking and stay off tobacco. In that community, an automated announcement is shared when members reach the anniversary of their successful quit date.

Temple. As far as I'm concerned, the websites themselves that bring members together online become temples as soon as members perceive others there with shared values who care about one another. The celebrations, from living with disease to launching companies, tell me that rituals are happening. As I mentioned earlier, even the most successful online managers know that members are enriched by offline meetings. When Stu and I talked, he didn't use the phrases "create a temporary temple" or "members pilgrimage" to meet one another, but that's how I interpreted his wisdom. Even online members want to go to a place where they can meet one another in a safe place where they do and say things that outsiders won't understand. It may be the most fun thing they do in the community.

Stories. Online members want to know the stories of the community and the stories of one another. Give them ways to learn those stories and to share their own, like with supplementing blog posts, videos, and interviews. Managers can highlight and feature stories that connect with the aspirational community values. My favorite examples are produced by the worldwide CrossFit headquarters. They post videos of personal lives transformed by their fitness community. The members' shared stories show how much that community values the most elite performers and the most novice. Remember, the stories you tell and the people you celebrate in them will reveal far more about who your community is than anything else.

Symbols. Symbols will emerge and will have their own meanings for every community. When you see them come up, you can embrace them, talk about them, and use them in rituals. I know of several online communities that have created badges to represent accomplishments, commitment levels, and service to the group. These badges can be seen by other members, and they're seen by members themselves when they return. The badges remind them of their commitment, values, and participation every visit.

Twitch is a very developed online community. It releases "emoticons" for its own community. I was moved when I learned how they're used and embraced by millions of users. One is called "Bible Thump." It depicts a character with tears running down its face. Marcus, director of programming at Twitch, explained that the emoticon is used to express empathy and sympathy. He said sometimes when something goes poorly for him on Twitch, his feed will turn into a "sea of Bible Thumps." It lets him know others care. The emoticon "POG Champ" is a photo of the face of Ryan Gutierrez, who, Marcus explained, is a well-known personality in the gaming community. POG Champ is shared to express excitement and surprise. Each symbol is understood by insiders and helps them connect in a tech-mediated forum.

Inner Rings

Inner rings are fairly easy to create online. Members can be invited to more exclusive groups separated by experience, location, or achievement. You can give different members different privileges that include leading discussions, posting in a special place, and mentoring members. Members will be excited to be recognized in a special way and privileged to serve and make a difference. When Kevin told me about some of the thousand members crying when Twitch invited them to become partners, I knew that this was because they wanted to be recognized for their contribution and be seen as important. I'm sure there was more that Twitch could do to involve members. Kevin had only scratched the surface.

Marcus explained that Twitch has many levels of inner rings, both formalized by Twitch and informally created by their users. I'll share some here so you can get a sense how these can work.

Members

Viewers: Over 100 million each month. Membership is often informally recognized when a viewer is recognized by a broadcaster.

Twitch Elders

Broadcasters: 1.7 million. They share content with Twitch on their own channel. Broadcaster CohhCarnage is a top-tier broadcaster, with 529,000 followers and over 27 million views.

Moderators: Each channel has designated moderators of their own choosing.

Influencers: Individuals who are prominent enough that they'll be offered paid opportunities to work with sponsors. This can include an invitation to broadcast from Twitch headquarters in San Francisco or to participate in sponsored events.

Partners: There are only fifteen hundred partners. They're given a "subscription button" that allows users to pay to follow them. Among other privileges, partners may create emoticons in the Twitch universe.

Global Moderators: They work to enforce community standards and rules of conduct.

Principal Elders

Twitch Support Team: Team members create and enforce the policies of the Twitch universe and can suspend or ban members.

Managing a Community

The art of managing and growing community could fill several books, much more than I can cover here. If you're interested, you may want to look into Elinor Ostrom's work. She's a Nobel Prize–winning economist who has identified eight features necessary to maintain a stable community property resource.[1] This wisdom applies to many of the communities you'll grow. While Ostrom's work overlaps with ideas I have already shared, it focuses more on long-term community management than on creating belonging and is worth exploring further for additional applications.

Features of a sustainable community:

First, there's a clear group identity with understood boundaries and purpose. Members know who is in or out and why they're together.

Second, benefits and costs are proportional. Members have a system that rewards contribution. Getting more benefits than others must be earned, or the group will collapse.

Third, decisions are made together. Members make decisions in a way they recognize is fair. This doesn't necessarily mean by consensus or simply by voting. It does mean that there's group participation.

Fourth, there's effective monitoring of violators or free riders. If members don't trust others to obey the rules, then they'll lose faith in the community.

Fifth, there are graduated sanctions for those who disrespect community rules. Small violations get small sanctions. Large violations get serious punishment.

Sixth, conflict-resolution mechanisms are inexpensive and easy to access. Conflicts can be handled quickly and in ways that members think is fair.

Seventh, there's recognition of some sort of rights to organize (for example, by the government). People must be allowed to organize for their own reasons. If they're forbidden to do so, that limits the third principle (making decisions together).

Eighth, for groups that are parts of bigger groups and networks, there must be coordination for relevant groups. Some activities are best handled in small groups, and some may require the involvement of many people. It's important that the right-size group—neither too big nor too small—handle whatever is at hand.

Discovering how Ostrom's principles apply to your situation will take time and will look different for each group. Her wisdom is an excellent starting place for those learning to manage large communities.

Epilogue: Endings and Beginnings

It's okay for a community to end. This can happen for any number of reasons: people move away, the goal is accomplished, interest has shifted away, other priorities arise, you can't serve members anymore. When a community ends, the relationships can continue. If we consider that the community's real purpose is to enrich members in some way, then it's okay if at some point a community stops gathering. You may not keep your temple, or enact your rituals, or use your symbols. With luck, you'll still have the relationships that were formed in your community, and this alone can be considered a success.

If you fear failure because your community is coming to an end, please know that ending doesn't necessarily mean failure. You may have simply created what was needed at the time, and now you get to start the next commitment. My favorite example of this was shared by my Neptune Studios friend Emily. She told me how she works on a film project for as long as three years and in that time she grows very close to her coworkers. By any standard, they become a community. They celebrate together, support one another in crises, and learn each other's stories. Once a film is finished, the team is inevitably broken up, and the members will go on to other film projects. She's been doing this for over ten years, so she's been through the cycle several times. It's not a matter of the community not working: its members have succeeded in creating what they set out to do, and their time has passed. She also shared how their relationships continue. She'll see those friends at the studio, perhaps on other projects, and they'll explore how they can work together again. They have joined new communities on new projects, and they're growing both professionally and personally in new ways.

Beginning with Acknowledgment

You may remember that I began this book by sharing that I went many years not knowing where I belonged. Another way to say the same thing is that I didn't yet feel as though I belonged where I was and with the people I knew. This is no longer the case. I would like to share with you the most powerful way I know that you can create belonging no matter who you are and where you're reading this book. As I mentioned in the beginning, community is formed when people believe they have mutual concern for one another. The fastest way I know to spark this sense of concern is to tell people that they matter to you. That's right, acknowledge people for the difference they make in your life. It's almost too easy an idea to believe that it works. I promise you it can. I'll share one way I use this idea.

I have a birthday tradition where I clear my calendar to make sure I do at least two things that day. The first is to write a letter to myself about what's happened in the past year, how I feel, and what I aspire to do in the future. This causes me to reflect on how I've spent my time and who's been involved. Then I make a list of the people who made a difference to me, and I call them one at a time, right down the list. My only goal in each call is to tell these individuals that I noticed what they did for me, how they made a difference, and that they matter in my life. Sometimes they've done really extraordinary things that saved me in a tough time. Sometimes they simply extended their friendship and made me feel welcome. I never exaggerate. I simply tell them that they made a difference to me. It looks something like this.

Melita,

I'm calling because today is my birthday.

This is a reflective time for me.

I look back on the past year and notice who fills my life
and makes it the adventure it actually is.

I'm calling because I want you to know that I both noticed
and it matters to me that

you invited me into your home.

You introduced us to your friends.

When I called with a big problem, you offered your professional perspective.

Without blinking an eye or asking anything of me.

You were very generous.

I think of you as someone I can call at any hour on any day
and you will be as supportive as you know how.

That makes a big difference to me
and it matters.

This is all I have to say.

Some friends tell me that these short calls changed their week
or came at a really hard time. Often I simply leave my message as
a voice mail and explain that they can call back, but it's not necessary. Some friends have done absolutely extraordinary things for
me (like Dr. Bennett, who built a spine board for my mother out of
jungle branches after an accident while she was traveling abroad).
For those friends, I honestly say, "I don't have words for how important our friendship is."

When I'm done making calls, a magical thing has happened.
More than two dozen people in my life know that they matter to
me, and I care about them. Some percentage of them tell me out-
right, "I feel the same way." Then I know there are people who care

about me. In a few hours I have a stronger community of support for my life. I truly believe that no matter what happens to me, I have people who want to help and know that I care about them. This is the most important community to me in the world. I don't need to be inside the world's other inner rings. They're only ancillary in my life.

If you want to create community right away, practice telling people who matter to you that they matter to you. When some of them tell you that you matter to them, well, then you have community. Then you get to grow it. You don't have to wait for your birthday. I've discovered any reason is a good one to tell people they matter. You can tell them that you read this book by an expert, and I told you to try it. But that isn't necessary. If you're stuck, you can use my simple structure below. If it doesn't work for you, then don't use it.

I'm calling because I'm noticing who makes my life better.
I thought of you.
I want you to know that I notice and appreciate that you . . . (thing they did)
This matters to me.
It makes a difference in my life.
This is all I wanted to share.

Most people never say these things. So when you do, it might sound weird, but *good* weird. I've never had someone get upset because I made this call. But there *are* a lot of people who feel newly appreciated and part of a stronger community.

Last Thought

Well, you did it. You got to the end, and you know more about how you can create belonging. I hope you're inspired. Very few people take the time to learn what you've just read. I think even fewer take a risk to use these ideas to connect to others and create "3 a.m. friends." If you do this, then you have my respect indeed. It won't always be fun. People won't always like you. You may feel silly many times. It is how the best parts of our lives are created.

Please remember that this book is offered as an inspiration with principles you can apply or refine when you are ready. It is no more than that. Your community can be great if it is growing members to be more generous, healthy, and supportive without matching each page I've shared.

I can't wait to learn what you create. I leave you with this wisdom that inspires me when I want to hold back because I'm tired, or feel weak or afraid:

> We have all known the long loneliness
> and we have learned that the only solution is love
> and that love comes with community.
> It all happened while we sat there talking,
> and it is still going on.
> — *Dorothy Day*

My team helps me create books, workshops, and community, and we would love to hear about your successes, failures, and challenges and how you're growing. We only do this to create a positive difference, and we only know if our efforts are making a difference if you tell us. The world is desperate for connection, and this is one way we can support it.

Go defeat loneliness. Create belonging. The world is waiting for it.

Godspeed.

You can reach both me and my team, find worksheets and other leader resources at charlesvogl.com.

Resources

Appendix A

Leader Worksheets

COMMUNITY LEADER WORKSHEET

This "next-steps" worksheet is for current or aspiring community leaders. Working through these steps will help you clarify what you intend to create and how to use the ideas in this book successfully. Remember, no matter how formal or informal your community prefers to be, the seven principles will likely become apparent over time, and, depending on how well they're introduced, they can help or hinder what you want to create.

You may not have answers to all these questions yet. This is perfectly fine. You may find some answers as soon as you look more deeply, while other answers may naturally emerge over time. In either case, knowing that these questions might come up will make a huge difference in creating clarity and strength.

Defining My Community

Communities must be defined at some level so that prospective members can know if they belong.

What is the name or description of our community?

(*Example: a community of Bay Area mountain biking enthusiasts.*)

Who is in our community now?

Who do we want in our community who is not yet in it?

Who should *not* be in our community?
(*Really, who doesn't share our values?*)

Values
What are the core values of our community?

How can we know these are the values?

How can other people (*current members as well as people interested in becoming members*) learn that these are our values?

Identity
Who does our community tell members we are? (*in any part of our lives*)

What does our community tell members we should do? (*about anything*)

What does our community tell members we should believe? (*about anything*)

Moral Proscriptions
What moral proscriptions in our community are different from those of others (*at least one person*) in the world?

What and whom do we protect?

What is unacceptable behavior?

What do we share? (*knowledge, objects, access*)

With whom do we share these things?

Whom do we particularly respect?

How do we show respect?

Understanding

What do our members want others to understand about them without having to explain themselves?

BOUNDARY WORKSHEET

Communities have a boundary between outsiders and insiders.

Insider Recognition

Do we know formally or informally who is in our community and who is outside? (*Even self-selecting communities have insiders and outsiders.*)

How do we know when someone is inside?

Boundary Invitation

Who are our gatekeepers who can welcome new members? (*informal or formal*)

How do newcomers find and access them?

Boundary Protection

Who maintains the boundary so that we know who is inside or outside? (*This can be several people, or just one, and can be informal or formal.*)

Has anyone ever been denied entry or rejected?

How was this enforced?

How do we prefer to enforce the boundary to protect the values in our community?

INITIATION WORKSHEET

Communities have an initiation ceremony of some kind, by which new members know that they are officially welcomed.

What is an activity that is understood as official recognition and welcome into the community? (*no matter how small*)

How can visitors become recognized as members?

How do they learn how to become a member?

Would members appreciate an option for a more ritualized initiation?

Initiation Ritual

Where do you prefer initiation to take place? (*if anywhere*)

What is/should be said?

Who leads or is present for the initiation?

Token

What item do you give members to take and remind them of their belonging?

Privileges

What privileges do members gain when welcomed inside the community? (*Closer connection, respect, more access, and understanding all count.*)

RITUAL WORKSHEET

Mature communities have rituals that honor important times or events.

Ritual Times

What activities are important rituals for the community? (*Even if unlabeled. Hint: if you changed the activities, members would feel the absence and be upset.*)

What events, transitions, or memorial moments do members appreciate are recognized by the community?

Community Display Ritual

When and how do members display their participation together so they can see others in the community?

Play Rituals

When do members play together as a community? (*Sporting events and celebrations count.*)

Format for Each Ritual

What activities do your members appreciate doing together that are special? (*Feasting, sporting, silence, singing, toasting all count.*)

What ritual tradition do you prefer to continue? (*if any*)

Who, preferably, is present?

Who preferably leads?

What preferably is said?

Token for Each Ritual
What do you pass on or leave behind to remember?

TEMPLE WORKSHEET

Mature communities have a special place where members gather and enact rituals. These can include play or honoring rituals.

Where do members gather to enact rituals? (*even play rituals*)

What is the most important place?

How do you make that place special when the community gathers?

Sacred Space
What spaces are special other than a main place?

When are these spaces special? (*for example, all the time or once a year or other frequency*)

How do you designate the spaces as special? (*Inviting people to the place for a specific time counts.*)

STORY WORKSHEET

Mature communities have stories by which they strengthen their identity and share values with newcomers.

Origin Stories

What origin story about the community do you want newcomers to know and understand?

Who was involved?

When was it?

What was the goal for the community?

What challenges were faced?

What was learned in creating the community?

Values Stories

What story do you want newcomers to understand that reveals how the community core values were upheld when facing a challenging time?

Vulnerable Stories

When did the community or certain members fail, and what important lesson(s) was learned?

Personal Stories

What personal stories about members would you want all members to learn?

How can members share their stories with others?

How can newcomers or visitors learn stories about members?

Sharing and Learning Stories

What opportunity can you create so members can share their own stories and hear stories important to your community?

SYMBOLS WORKSHEET

What are the most important symbols for your community and what do they represent?

Who uses them and how are they used?

How did they become symbols?

What tokens do/could members keep and what meaning do/could they hold?

INNER RING WORKSHEET

What are the names for the inner rings in your community and the privileges for each? (*Please do not create new inner rings that aren't helpful.*)

Visitor
Novice
Member
Elder
Principal Elder

How do members enter the inner rings?

How do members learn the path to inner rings?

How do senior members show their concern beyond themselves?

The diaconate holds authority in these areas:

> Protecting the boundary
> Officiating at rituals
> Teaching community values

Who represents the diaconate in your community? (*They are probably called something else, and may even have no title.*)

How do members know that those people are the diaconate?

How can others join the diaconate?

How do you know whose contribution is valued more than others?

ADVANCED IDEA: LEADING GROWTH WORKSHEET

Mature communities teach members to succeed at something they want (making supportive friends counts).

What do your members want to succeed at? (*Creating safe, deep, and connected friendships counts. So does learning a skill.*)

What outward skills are they learning (informally or formally)? (*How to be a supportive neighbor, support new friends, and make a safe neighborhood count.*)

How do they learn?

What wisdom are they learning about internal mental and emotional health?

How do members understand something is not as it seems to outsiders?

You can get downloads of worksheets and examples filled by community leaders at charlesvogl.com

Take It to the Community

Once you as a leader have completed the worksheet in as much detail as you can, you should have new ideas about your community and how you can strengthen it. The next step is to take those ideas to your members, or to those who you think want to be your members, and ask them for their thoughts. I promise that you'll be surprised! And you'll probably be shocked by how much they'll appreciate an honest, values-based, and welcoming effort to strengthen their community.

You can reach both me and my team at charlesvogl.com.

Appendix B

Dinner Community Case Study

This case study shows how I used a set of worksheets to pose questions about the seven principles in the Prospect Street dinner community I helped create. Your answers should reflect you, not the dinner community.

Prospect Dinners Introduction

When I first arrived at Yale in 2007, the woman who's now my wife, Socheata, and I moved into a small townhouse on Prospect Street. We had been living in New York for about six years and knew virtually no one in New Haven.

Years earlier, I had met Lolita Jackson, a wise and experienced political coalition builder, who has now served in senior positions with successive New York mayors. This is unusual for anyone, even more so for an African American woman. Lolita taught me the importance of scheduling time to invite others to "intimate experiences." She explained to me that meeting people at parties, hanging out with them at bars, and saying "Hi" to them at conferences didn't count toward creating deep and meaningful relationships. There's nothing wrong with meeting at large events, she said, but *intimate* experiences are what builds a relationship. This is true in religion, politics, business, and life.

At some level, Lolita explained, this wisdom comes down to math. The number of real friendships you'll create is related to some function of how many intimate experiences you create. To create experiences, you have to schedule them. You have to prioritize them in your life, understanding that these experiences can deliver what you want—a group of friends who would stand together in tough times, enjoy the calm times, and celebrate the happy times. More important, it would create social change by collecting skills, wisdom, access, money, and strength that can be found only in community.

I also wanted to live the wisdom of C. S. Lewis and escape the never-ending cycle of the inner ring. He said that the way to escape this was by engaging in something you liked to do and inviting others to join you in it regularly. He predicted that, by doing this, we would create that which we sought. We would create friendships that to outsiders might look like an inner ring, but would be something else entirely because anyone sharing the values could join. The friendships would free us from the pursuit of the inner ring.

Combining their wisdom, Socheata and I had been hosting dinners for one or two guests in our tiny Queens apartment about twice a week for years. We developed some of our closest friendships this way. Now in New Haven, we had a slightly bigger home, and we could invite a larger number of people. We visited thrift stores until we gathered enough plates, glasses, serving dishes, serving spoons, and all the other stuff needed to host at least twelve people.

In the first week of my first semester, I sent out an invitation to my whole department, inviting anyone who would like to join us to share dinner on Friday night. Socheata and I made a feast. As I recall it, about eighteen people came, mostly strangers to us.

We could not sit around our table, and so we spilled over onto our floor. Everyone wanted to make new friends.

It looked like instant success, but in the next six weeks or so I discovered a problem. Once the novelty of our dinners wore off, attendance dropped sharply. There were many things to do on Friday nights at Yale, and our home didn't offer a lot of drama. Soon I didn't know whether ten people, or only four, would join us. I never knew how much to cook or exactly when our surprise guests would arrive. In any case, I'd have to spend a good five hours shopping for and preparing a meal.

I began asking for RSVPs, so that I would know how many to expect. It was disappointing when friends would tell me they would join us, I would cook for hours, and then, just before dinner, they would choose a better option for their evening. It was so easy to cancel on this week's free dinner when they knew there would be another next week. After enough last-minute cancellations, I began to question my worth. I wondered if what I was doing was worth the time, the grocery bills, and the personal risk inviting so many people, most of whom turned me down or ignored me week after week. I wondered who thought I was a loser because I'd invite so often and most would never come. It was lots of work, and not a lot of fun.

Sometime in the second semester, the stream of RSVPs and cancellations and the racing to fill canceled seats got to be too much. I created an online RSVP system so I wouldn't have to respond to every request or cancellation myself. That week two friends told me that they didn't want to be invited anymore because, with a sign-up system, it was now too "institutionalized." Apparently, they preferred that I shop, cook, host, and personally note each cancellation and RSVP.

Still, the numbers grew, and our little dinner series became a bit famous and full. Some friends returned often enough to know where we kept our kitchen gear and how we set up, and of course they helped clean up after the meal. They were our regulars and a huge help. As the third year began, I knew we couldn't continue as we had started. Serving a four-course feast for twelve to fourteen people every Friday night was exhausting and took up a big part of our lives. Those first two years, Socheata and I shopped for and cooked each meal. If we were to continue, we would need help.

One sunny fall afternoon, an invited group of our regulars sat in the Divinity School common room to invent a whole new system to continue the now robust dinner series. They loved the friendships and community that the series had created as much as we did. We decided that each of us would take responsibility for two dinners a semester as dinner leaders. We would each recruit the volunteers needed for our own dinners. In time, volunteers would grow to lead dinners themselves. Gradually, the dinners got better and better, as the new leaders brought their own heritage and fresh enthusiasm. Many hosts made old family recipes to share at their dinners. On two occasions, mothers were brought in from far away to help host and create family recipes.

We lived a bit more than a mile away from the central downtown Yale campus. Undergraduates had to either walk half an hour each way or take the campus shuttle to join us. Either option took about an hour round-trip. Nonetheless, about half of our guests were Yale undergraduates! This surprised me because Yale undergraduates have no fewer than twelve dining halls available to them each evening with organic salad bars, fresh-made desserts, and even brick-oven pizza. They all had prepaid credit for every meal. I wondered why they were spending so much time on a Friday night to join us.

One day, Courtney, one of our leaders, told me she was on campus talking on the phone about our dinner series. When she hung up, another Yale student approached her and, with the enthusiasm of discovering secret knowledge, asked if she attended "the dinners on Prospect Street." The student wanted to know how she could get an invitation. We laughed about this. That was the day that I learned we had in fact created what Lewis had predicted. In two years, we had created what looked like an exclusive inner ring at Yale, even though our intention was to invite anyone who wanted to join us and share a sit-down meal.

I learned that in the social landscape of both undergraduate and graduate students at Yale, the number of occasions where they are invited to sit down for three to five hours, share a meal, and get to know others with no agenda is about zero. That the number of places where faculty, staff, or students can share deep conversation with someone outside their departments is also very small. At our dinners, we also included friends from outside the university and even strangers who somehow discovered us on their own.

I also learned that the concept of hosting a four-course sit-down meal, inviting strangers at no charge and with no hidden agenda, stretched the bounds of credulity for many. One fall, I got a phone call from a graduate student who asked me many times where exactly the dinners were hosted. I was confused because the location was specified on the registration site. Eventually I understood that she didn't believe we were simply hosting a meal in our home to build friendship. She was convinced it was a secret bait-and-switch recruitment event, and she wanted to know what organization was hosting it. She hung up still angry because I wouldn't reveal who was "really" running the show.

Within three years, there were few places on campus Socheata and I could go where someone didn't know us as the hosts of the dinner series. Without question, the dinners became the founding place for some of our dearest friendships. Friendships created over a dinner table can and do change the lives of guests.

One night, an undergraduate I'll call Janice met my friends

Eric and Jane, who were both preparing for ordination as Episcopal priests. I didn't know as I listened to their conversation that Eric and Jane were the first liberal social justice Christians with whom Janice had ever shared a conversation. In meeting Eric and Jane, she discovered a Christian world that was more welcoming and inclusive than she had thought Christianity could be. The conversation that night began her journey to come out as gay to her conservative Christian parents, and led her to found the first LGBTQ undergraduate social group in Yale's three-hundred-year history.

About half the time, undergraduate students led our dinners. More often than not, they had no experience in preparing a dinner party for fourteen with multiple courses. In almost every case, they overestimated what they could cook and how quickly. These were near-disasters, although we tried to keep the standards high. I remember when one student got only about half of his meal prepared and frantically tried to complete more in a kitchen strewn with ingredients and dirty dishes. In that moment, I got an insight. While trying to help the student clean up before he began the next dish, I realized that we were doing far more than just serving meals and offering a space for friendship. We were training the next generation on how to be great hosts. I realized that many friends were coming to learn how to *do* this, and not just to experience it.

In the fourth year, our friend Arjan agreed to coordinate the leaders so I didn't have to schedule dates or create guest lists and volunteer rosters. He did a far better job than I did. The following year, Sam took over the coordinating role and refined our system even more. Serving hundreds of people, the series ran more smoothly and had more smart, committed minds shaping it.

Since leaving Yale, I still hear stories about how those dinners changed the lives of our guests. One friend, who has an important position at Google, has told me that although he attended our dinners only twice, they're among the highlights of his experience at Yale. Another friend has told me that everything in his life that he loves he attributes to knowing us (really!). The relationships he made in our home and community opened doors to the life that he has now, including meeting his now wife. Lydia told me she credits dating her now husband as quickly as she did because she got to know him at our dinner table.

This dinner series ended when we all left the university. But our relationships continue as we have spread around the globe, and some of our members have begun their own gatherings in their new home towns. May the friendships continue.

PROSPECT DINNERS WORKSHEETS EXAMPLE

Defining My Community

Communities must be defined at some level so prospective members can know if they belong (or want to run away).

What is the name or description of our community?

Prospect Dinners (or Friday Night Candlelight Dinners at Yale). We are people who like to cook and share long dinners together without distractions in order to build new friendships and deepen others.

Who is in our community?

People who live in or near New Haven. Mostly people who work or study at Yale, though there are exceptions.

Who do we want in our community who is not yet in it?

There are many in and around New Haven whom we would like to include. This includes others who value sharing dinners and conversation to build friendship. They may feel lonely or simply want to find others who seek deep friendships. They understand the value of participating with others to create a special, respectful space for friendship.

Who should *not* be in our community?

Those who prioritize a Friday evening to get drunk, be entertained, impress others, or escape in media. Those who are prioritizing a free meal. Those who prioritize dinner parties to show off culinary feats more than create friendship. Those who create a distraction from the goal of the event. Those who cannot be trusted to be respectful or safe in a stranger's home.

Values

What are core values of our community?

Our lives are deeply enriched by creating these things:

> *Deep friendship*
> *Honest and thoughtful conversation about ideas*
> *Creating a special protected space for welcoming others*
> *Inviting strangers to know us and one another*

How can we know these are the values?

Deep friendship: We listen to one another and offer support for challenges and goals.

Honest conversation: We create conversations for three to four hours each week.

Special welcome space: We set up a special place each week and welcome strangers to join us.

Inviting strangers: We make participation available to strangers. We encourage participants to invite anyone they like.

How can other people (current members as well as people interested in becoming members) learn that these are our values?

They can see how we create activities consistent with our values above. They can see the values explicitly referenced in our invitations. We reference these values at the beginning of each of our dinners.

Identity

Who does our community tell members we are? (*in any part of our lives*)

We are people who are looking for connection. We are people who enrich others by offering friendship. We are generous in our invitations and with our time.

What does our community tell members we should do? (*about anything*)

Spend time with strangers. Share long undisturbed conversations with others. Build new friendships to enrich our lives.

What does our community tell members we should believe? (*about anything*)

Welcoming and hosting others is important and generous. Meeting strangers and spending time with them is fun and important. Presenting a dinner party is far less important than the relationships that form at the dinner party. Friendships make our lives and those around us far more fun and powerful.

Beliefs

What must full members believe to participate?

Sharing a meal together is a powerful tool to create and strengthen relationships.

Cooperating to host dinners is important.

Long, patient conversations are important and enrich lives.

Meeting new people, listening, and sharing are important and enriching.

Moral Proscriptions

What moral proscriptions in our community are different from those of others (*at least one person*) in the world?

It is important to invite strangers.

It is important to give all guests an opportunity to share equally.

It is important to talk about things that matter.

It is important to be vulnerable when creating a relationship.

It is important to honor hosts and guests by being on time.

What and whom do we protect?

We protect the ritual space and time for friendship building.

We protect the hopes, dreams, and potential of people in our space.

We protect those who extend themselves to present a meal and create a welcoming event.

What is unacceptable behavior?

Reserving space and not showing up without communication.

Attacking others at the dinner.

Committing to deliver an item or service and not delivering.

Eating and leaving without participating in conversation.

What do we share? (*knowledge, objects, access*)

Food

Time

Conversation

Knowledge

Friendship and community-building wisdom

Dinner party hosting skills and wisdom

With whom do we share these things?

People in, near, and visiting New Haven who want to join strangers for a dinner and build friendships.

Whom do we particularly respect?

The volunteers who fund and do the work to present the gift of a meal to strangers.

How do we show respect?

We offer help. We invite them to events first. We invite them to private events and meals where there are no outsiders.

Understanding

What do our members want others to understand about them without having to explain themselves?

We are looking for friendship.

We want to be friends.

We want to be generous.

We want to share of ourselves by offering food.

We want to welcome others.

We want to know others in ways that can only happen with long conversations.

BOUNDARY WORKSHEET

Communities have a boundary between outsiders and insiders.

Insider Recognition

Do we know formally or informally who is in our community and who is outside? (*Even self-selecting communities have insiders and outsiders.*)

Membership is mostly informal. However, members who volunteer more than once, lead a dinner, or sponsor a dinner are clearly on the inside.

How do we know when someone is inside?

For informal members, that they attend at least three dinners and volunteer during the event.

Boundary Invitation

Who are our gatekeepers who can welcome new members? (*informal or formal*)

Any dinner leader or coordinator is a gatekeeper.

How do newcomers find and access them?

There are dinner leaders at each dinner. They are always identified and acknowledged.

Boundary Protection

Who maintains the boundary so that we know who is inside or outside? (*This can be several people, or just one, and can be informal or formal.*)

Socheata and I maintain the boundary. The series is hosted in our home. We can exclude anyone we like.

Has anyone ever been denied entry or rejected?

Yes. Anyone who registers for a dinner spot and then does not show up and never communicates about this is denied a spot in the future. We reserve space for those who show up for the prepared meals.

How was this enforced?

I told them they are not allowed to reserve another spot.

How do we prefer to enforce the boundary to protect the values in our community?

Any dinner leader or I can tell any visitor or member what is not permitted or when they may not attend.

STORY WORKSHEET

Mature communities have stories by which they strengthen their identity and share values with newcomers.

Origin Stories

What origin story about the community do you want newcomers to know and understand?

We want visitors to know that Socheata and I began the series in our first weeks in New Haven, in part inspired by C. S. Lewis's inner ring wisdom. That we cooked all the meals for the first two years and that it became too difficult. That volunteers then took over most of the meals to welcome strangers from across Yale and New Haven to enjoy the time together.

Who was involved?

Socheata and I began the series. Lydia, James, Courtney, and Bjorn were early volunteers. Arjan took on coordinating all the dinners when they became too much.

When was it?

We began in August 2007.

What was the goal for the community?

To build diverse friendships that would enrich our lives and support us to create a greater impact for the rest of our lives.

What challenges were faced?

It was difficult to figure out how to invite people so that others would understand what we were doing, how to plan for the size of the dinners, how to invite enough volunteers, and how many hours it took to prepare the meals each week.

What was learned in creating the community?

We must be explicit that the relationships are far more important than the food.

We are teaching people how to host powerful dinner parties as much as we are hosting them.

Many people feel lonely and long for a specific time to make deep connections.

Values Stories

What story do you want newcomers to understand that reveal how the community core values were upheld when facing a challenging time?

Exploding Pyrex
The story about the time Scott exploded a Pyrex dish in the oven during the meal. That was when we understood that the gear that we use for the gatherings was simply there to be used. Breaking things is to be expected when hosting so many events. The experience is far more important than the equipment.

Ribs Night
The story about Jake making southern ribs for dinner and offering the lone vegetarian guest a microwaved veggie patty. This is the night we learned that we needed to honor every guest with a great meal and ensure that there was a good vegetarian option at every dinner.

Vulnerable Stories

When did the community or certain members fail, and what important lesson (or lessons) was learned?

Dumplings
The evening Jane and Phil could not feed everyone because they planned a meal that took too long to prepare was very disappointing. We learned that we needed to have patience with hosts who were themselves learning how to host, and that we needed to spend more time with them preparing what they planned to create. We needed to invest in training and supporting our hosts so they would commit only to what they could create.

Personal Stories

What personal stories about members would you want all members to learn?

Charles and Socheata cooked all the dinners in the series for the first two years.

How Janice learned there were Christian communities that accept her for being gay.

How James met David over the dinners and they both went to Uganda to work for an orphanage that James founded.

How James and Lydia bonded over the dinners and then married.

How can members share their stories with others?

Over dinner conversation. And during the shopping and meal preparation time. Stories are also shared during kitchen cleanup.

How can newcomers or visitors learn stories about members?

Over dinner conversation when time is specifically left available for any subject.

Sharing and Learning Stories

What opportunity can you create so members can share their own stories and hear stories important to your community?

We could create a blog so visitors could submit their own stories.

We could include a link to these stories in our invitations.

INITIATION WORKSHEET

Communities have an initiation ceremony of some kind, by which new members know that they are officially welcomed.

What is an activity that is understood as official recognition and welcome into the community? (*no matter how small*)

Listening to the wisdom about escaping the trap of the inner ring by creating friendship.

How can visitors become recognized as members?

They are explicitly recognized when they volunteer to present a dinner for others.

How do they learn how to become a member?

All guests are invited to contact the coordinator and offer to volunteer or lead a dinner if they are so inspired.

Would members appreciate an option for a more ritualized initiation?

Yes. It would be stronger to officially give permission for members to invite their own guests to the dinners. This could include a handmade card that they can share with others as an invitation.

Initiation Ritual

Where do you prefer initiation to take place? (*if anywhere*)
In the space where we host dinners.

What should be said?

Acknowledgment for their commitment to make a space for others to create connection.

Reminder that making change in the world takes a community. We who make up community are building the muscles and the tools to create profound change.

Reminder that we do all of this to change lives for the rest of our lives and for more people than we will ever know.

Permission to invite others to join the dinner.

Who leads or is present for the initiation?
The dinner coordinator or founding host

At least one dinner leader

Token

What item do you give members to take and remind them of their belonging?

We will need to ask members what they think would symbolize the community well.

One idea is two pair of handmade chopsticks because they symbolize coming together and sharing a meal.

Another idea is a candle holder to represent preparing a welcome table for others.

Privileges

What privileges do members gain when welcomed inside the community? (*Closer connection, respect, more access, and understanding all count.*)

They get closer connection with other members.

They get trained on hosting dinner parties to build connection.

They may invite anyone they like to join a dinner.

They have access to the members contact list.

They get to participate in a tribe bigger than themselves.

RITUAL WORKSHEET

Mature communities have rituals that honor important times or events.

Ritual Times

What activities are important rituals for the community? (*Even if unlabeled. Hint: if you changed the activities, members would feel their absence and be upset.*)

The opening dinner ritual

Gathering around the table for the welcome

Identifying first-time visitors

Sharing the series tradition history

Referencing Lewis's inner ring

Sharing the series intention to create friendship

Sharing the menu

Inviting the leader to share a prayer in any language and tradition that is their own

Changing seats before the dessert course

Sitting down again for dessert presentation

Serving a chocolate, fruit, and tea course so guests know they can stay

What events, transitions, or memorial moments do members appreciate are recognized by the community?

Visiting parents, family, or friends

Success in school applications, job offers, fellowship awards, and so forth

Struggles with medical or academic challenges

Community Display Ritual

When and how do members display their participation together so they can see others in the community?

The dinners themselves are displays of participation together.
The menu planning, shopping, and meal preparation are all done privately.

Play Rituals

When do members play together as a community? (*sporting events and celebrations count*)

The dinners are a kind of play. There are private events like concerts, pie making, and house parties where members also gather for celebration.

Format for Each Ritual

What activities do your members appreciate doing together that are special? (*Feasting, sporting, silence, singing, toasting all count.*)

Cooking

Eating

Sunday lunch

What ritual tradition do you prefer to continue? (*if any*)

The opening dinner ritual is very important to continue to offer solemnity and intention to the event.

Who, preferably, is present?

Leader

Volunteer

New guests

Who preferably leads?

Dinner leader for the evening

What preferably is said?

Welcoming

Sharing the series tradition

Referencing Lewis's inner ring

Sharing the intention of the evening to create friendship

Token for Each Ritual

What do you pass on or leave behind to remember?

Right now we only offer memories and invitations for the future. We could make the experience more powerful by offering a token for guests and members to take with them. This could be a set of handmade chopsticks or a pendant of a Maltese dog. The Maltese reference can be useful because our Maltese attends each dinner and is a big feature for university students without pets. Further, she is mentioned in each dinner invitation.

TEMPLE WORKSHEET

Mature communities have a special place where members gather and enact rituals. These can include play or honoring rituals.

Where do members gather to enact rituals? (*even play rituals*)
At our home on Prospect Street

What is the most important place?
Our home on Prospect Street

How do you make that place special when the community gathers?
The space is cleaned and garbage removed.

A dining table is set up to accommodate exactly the number of guests registered.

At least one candle per guest is lit on the table.

A meal of at least four courses is prepared for serving.

The lights are dimmed.

Sacred Space

What spaces are special other than a main place?
None come to mind.

When are these spaces special? (*for example, all the time or once a year or other frequency*)

At least once a week. Other times we gather for impromptu meals or dessert together. The space is also used to celebrate birthdays, success, and failure.

How do you designate the spaces as special? (*Inviting people to the place for a specific time counts.*)
Invitations go out.

The space is cleaned.

A fresh meal is prepared.

SYMBOLS WORKSHEET

What are the most important symbols for your community?
Gathering around the table and sitting down in unison

The candles on the table

The set table

Our Maltese dog, "Friday"

Slippers (offered to each guest when they arrive)

What do they represent? (*Each will represent several things.*)
Gathering around the table and sitting down in unison: patience and presence

Welcoming

Generosity

Play and fun

Preparation

A sacred gathering

Who uses them, and how are they used?
All items are used to prepare the space for an event.

The dog was mentioned in every invitation and offered for cuddling to all guests.

How did they become symbols?
They were used for years.

They were distinctive elements of our dinner series.

What tokens do/could members keep and what meaning do/could they hold?
Handmade card that could be used to invite others

Candle

A distinctive serving bowl or other service piece to use in the future

What could they could mean?
Membership in a community and a ritual that matters

Generosity

Welcome

Play and fun

INNER RING WORKSHEET

What are the names for the inner rings in your community and the privileges for each? (*Please don't create new inner rings that aren't helpful.*)

Visitor: Guests who participate in the dinner series

Novice: Guests who participate in the dinner series

Member: Volunteers who learn how the series is created and invite guests

Elder: Dinner leaders who select a menu, choose volunteers, and invite guests with priority access

Senior Elder: Coordinators who can veto the menu and give access to the venue to anyone

Principal Elder: Founding hosts who protect the boundary, shape the ritual, choose priorities, and can veto the menu

How do members enter the inner rings?
They tell any dinner leader, coordinator, or host that they want to become more involved.

How do members learn the path to inner rings?
They can be informed by the coordinator or the hosts.

How do senior members show their concern beyond themselves?
Senior members not only care that they have a good time but that all the guests have a good time. They will do any task that is needed for success.

DIACONATE WORKSHEET

The diaconate holds authority in these areas: policing the boundary, officiating at rituals, and teaching community values.

Who represents the diaconate in your community? (*They are probably called something else, and may even have no title.*)

Charles and Socheata

Sam

Arjan

How do members know that those people are the diaconate?
Charles and Socheata are the hosts.

Sam and Arjan are identified as the coordinators on the registration website and at the events.

How can others join the diaconate?

They participate enough that they are trusted to run the operation. If they ask to have more responsibility, it can be given by any of the diaconate.

How do you know whose contribution is valued more than others?

Charles and Socheata host the events in their own home. They choose what can and cannot happen.

ADVANCED IDEA: LEADING GROWTH WORKSHEET

Mature communities teach members to succeed at something they want (making supportive friends counts).

What do your members want to succeed at? (*Creating safe, deep and connected friendships counts. So does learning a skill.*)

Make deep friendship

Host meaningful dinner parties

Learn dinner host etiquette

What outward skills are they learning? (*informally or formally*) (*How to be a supportive neighbor, support new friends, and make a safe neighborhood count.*)

Cooking

Table setting

Scheduling

Tea making

How do they learn?

Working alongside more experienced members

Experimenting

Reading online resources provided by the community

What wisdom are they learning about internal mental and emotional health?

Hosting is about sharing welcome and dignity far more than about serving food.

Preparing a special place takes time and patience.

Keeping personal integrity is critical to making a space others want to enter.

How do members understand something is not as it seems to outsiders?

Dinner parties are not successful because the food, decorations, and invitations are elaborate or expensive. They are successful because the host makes a space where each person is expected and a special place is prepared for them.

The dinners are meaningful because the host offers an intention about relationships and gives permission to talk about important topics, fears, loves, and hopes.

Notes

Preface

1. C. S. Lewis, "The Inner Ring," Memorial Lecture, King's College, University of London, 1944.
2. Miller McPherson, Lynn Smith-Lovin, and Matthew E. Brashears, "Social Isolation in America: Changes in Core Discussion Networks over Two Decades," *American Sociological Review* 71, no. 3 (2006): 353–75.
3. "Relationships Boost Survival by 50 Percent," *Scientific American*, July 28, 2010, www.scientificamerican.com/article/relationships-boost-survival.
4. "Nones on the Rise," Pew Research on Religion and Public Life, October 9, 2012, www.pewforum.org/2012/10/09/nones-on-the-rise/.
5. Ibid.
6. DDB Needham Life Style Surveys, 1975–99, quoted in Robert Putnam, "Bowling Alone: The Collapse and Revival of American Community," *Journal of Democracy* 6, no. 1 (1995): 65–7
7. John R. Robinson and Geoffrey Godbey, *Time for Life: The Surprising Ways Americans Use Their Time*, 2nd ed. (University Park: Pennsylvania State University Press, 1999).
8. DDB Needham Life Style Surveys.
9. *Millennials: Breaking the Myths*, Nielsen, nielsen.com, January 27, 2014.

10. *The 2013 Millennial Impact Report*, Achieve, achieveguidance.com, 2013.

11. *Fifteen Economic Facts about Millennials*, Council of Economic Advisors, whitehouse.gov, October 2014.

12. *Inspiring the Next Generation: The 2014 Millennial Impact Report*, Achieve, casefoundation.org, 2014.

13. Quoted in Robert Waldinger, "The Good Life," TEDxBeaconStreet, November 30, 2015.

14. J. Holt-Lunstad, T. B. Smith, and J. B. Layton, "Social Relationships and Mortality Risk: A Meta-analytic Review," *PLoS Med* 7, no. 7 (2010), e1000316, doi:10.1371/journal.pmed.1000316.

15. Seth Godin, *Tribes: We Need You to Lead Us* (London: Penguin, 2008), 24.

Chapter 1 Understanding Community

1. Putnam, "Bowling Alone," 71.

2. Stephanie Cooperman, "Getting Fit, Even If It Kills You," *New York Times*, December 22, 2005.

3. Mark Oppenheimer, "When Some Turn to Church, Others Go to CrossFit," *New York Times*, November 27, 2015.

4. Christie Aschwanden, "An Insider's Guide to CrossFit," *New York Times* (blog), August 18, 2014, http://well.blogs.nytimes.com/2014/08/18/crossfit-book-breathe-fire/?_r=0.

Chapter 2: The Boundary Principle

1. Yascha Mounk, "Is Harvard Unfair to Asian-Americans?," *New York Times*, November 24, 2014.

2. Ibid.

Chapter 4: The Rituals Principle

1. Roy Baumeister, Kathleen Vohs, Jennifer Aaker, and Emily Garbinsky, "Some Key Differences between a Happy Life and a Meaningful Life," *Journal of Positive Psychology* 8, no. 6 (2013): 505–16.

2. Excerpts from the speech by International Olympic Committee president Thomas Bach, opening ceremony, 126th session, Sochi, February 4, 2014 (slightly modified).

3. Excerpts from the speech by International Olympic Committee president Jacques Rogge, opening ceremony, London Olympic Games, July 28, 2012 (slightly modified).

Chapter 6: The Stories Principle

1. Brené Brown, *Daring Greatly: How the Courage to Be Vulnerable Transforms the Way We Live, Love, Parent, and Lead* (New York: Gotham Books, 2012), 37.

Chapter 8: The Inner Rings Principle

1. Interview with Lama Surya Das, February 26, 2016, www.surya.org.
2. Lewis, "Inner Ring."
3. I'm taking this term from ancient Christian tradition and using it slightly differently. The Diaconate is the official body of Deacons. The term *deacon* comes from the ancient Greek word *diakonos*, which means "servant." Deacons serve the church body.
4. A. H. Maslow, *Toward a Psychology of Being* (New York: Van Nostrand, 1968).
5. Roy F. Baumeister and Mark R. Leary, "The Need to Belong: Desire for Interpersonal Attachments as a Fundamental Human Motivation," *Psychological Bulletin* 117 (1995): 497–529.
6. S. E. Asch, "Effects of Group Pressure upon the Modification and Distortion of Judgment," in *Groups, Leadership, and Men*, edited by H. Guetzkow (Pittsburgh, PA: Carnegie Press, 1951).
7. Alfred Adler, quoted in Gina Stepp, "A Psychology of Change," *Vision* (Winter 2011), www.vision.org/visionmedia/alfred-adler-adlerian-psychology/41045.aspx.
8. Carolyn Schwartz, Janice Bell Meisenhelder, Yunsheng Ma, and George Reed, "Altruistic Social Interest Behaviors Are Associated with Better Mental Health," *Psychosomatic Medicine* 65, no. 5 (2003): 778–85.
9. W. T. Harbaugh, U. Myer, and D. R. Burghart, "Neural Responses to Taxation and Voluntary Giving Reveal Motives for Charitable Donations," *Science* 316, no. 5831 (2007): 1622–25.
10. Baumeister, Vohs, Aaker, and Garbinsky, "Key Differences between a Happy Life and a Meaningful Life."

Chapter 10: Managing Community Face-to-Face and Online

1. Elinor Ostrom, *Governing the Commons: The Evolution of Institutions for Collective Action* (Cambridge: Cambridge University Press, 1990).

Last Thoughts

The quotation from Dorothy Day appears in *The Long Loneliness: The Autobiography of Dorothy Day* (Garden City, N.Y.: Image Books, 1959), p. 286.

Acknowledgments

Several people supported me on this adventure so much that I am humbled, emboldened, and inspired to have them alongside me. Dai Sun and Betty Chang, Bjorn Cooley, Gabriel Grant, Jason Harp, Kurt Johnson, Emily Levada, Rose-Anne Moore, Eric Ng, Mike O'Malley, Socheata Poeuv, Alan Price, Scott Sherman, and Friday Dog, who sat with me through so many words. You make all the difference and I notice.

Many people were generous with their time and experience in creating this book: Patricia Alejandro, Melissa Allen, Philip Armand, Lama Surya Das, Judith Dupre, Amit Garg, Marcus Graham, Joel Grant, Lolita Jackson, Glenn Libby, Kevin Lin, Elizabeth Marshman, Stu McLaren, Mike Minium, Liz Morgan, Sara Newens, Alastair Ong, Bruce Quan, Nathana Sharma, James Vogl, Katie Wallace, Adam Warheit, Rebecca Wexler, Ben Winegarden, Josh Wyner.

The kind people at the café on 40th Street who let me camp out with my computer. You really helped when I needed a place to go.

And those who shared their experiences with me and prefer to keep their identity private.

Please accept my deep appreciation.

Index

About the Author

Charles Vogl is an author and executive consultant. He works with leaders in tech, finance, media, government, and social change organizations to make meaningful change. This work includes helping others inspire powerful connections in critical relationships. He draws from the realm of spiritual traditions to understand how individuals build loyalty, strengthen identity, and live  out shared values. These principles apply to both secular and spiritual leadership. He believes that every influential leader builds a community of stakeholders and crucial relationships on whom they depend. When leaders know how to create a robust and committed community, they create relationships that are effective and resilient. These relationships deliver when needed most and create profound change.

Charles got his introduction in community building as a twenty-four-year-old full-time volunteer with a radical homeless shelter in Santa Ana, California. There he was stunned by the compassion and commitment of activists doing thankless and nauseating work in the face of seemingly overwhelming need. They could continue only by serving in community. He went on to work on rural health care access and human rights as a US Peace Corps volunteer in Zambia, where he was mostly exhausted, ineffective, and overwhelmed trying to make a difference.

It was only later as a struggling documentary filmmaker in New York that new mentors taught him the importance and philosophy of building community for change. For the first time, his work and team achieved international success. The training was critically important when he volunteered as a New York restaurant labor organizer after experiencing worker abuse himself. That campaign changed the national labor law landscape to newly empower abused restaurant workers. He went on to study leaders in political and social movements and spiritual traditions at Yale University. He guest lectures at the Yale Leadership Institute and Yale School of Management. He co-instructed the first Yale University social entrepreneurship course with Dr. Scott Sherman.

He has a BS from the USC Annenberg School and a Master of Divinity from Yale University where he studied ethics, religion, philosophy, and business. He was also named a Jesse Ball DuPont Foundation Scholar. He lives in beautiful Oakland, California, with his wife, Socheata Poeuv, and a rescued Maltese dog. In one year he also survived a plane crash, a spitting cobra attack, and acute malaria.

On most weekends he prefers making a hot meal with and for friends with a lot of laughter throughout.

You can contact him at charlesvogl.com.

Berrett–Koehler
BK Publishers

Berrett-Koehler is an independent publisher dedicated to an ambitious mission: *connecting people and ideas to create a world that works for all*.

We believe that to truly create a better world, action is needed at all levels—individual, organizational, and societal. At the individual level, our publications help people align their lives with their values and with their aspirations for a better world. At the organizational level, our publications promote progressive leadership and management practices, socially responsible approaches to business, and humane and effective organizations. At the societal level, our publications advance social and economic justice, shared prosperity, sustainability, and new solutions to national and global issues.

A major theme of our publications is "Opening Up New Space." Berrett-Koehler titles challenge conventional thinking, introduce new ideas, and foster positive change. Their common quest is changing the underlying beliefs, mindsets, institutions, and structures that keep generating the same cycles of problems, no matter who our leaders are or what improvement programs we adopt.

We strive to practice what we preach—to operate our publishing company in line with the ideas in our books. At the core of our approach is stewardship, which we define as a deep sense of responsibility to administer the company for the benefit of all of our "stakeholder" groups: authors, customers, employees, investors, service providers, and the communities and environment around us.

We are grateful to the thousands of readers, authors, and other friends of the company who consider themselves to be part of the "BK Community." We hope that you, too, will join us in our mission.

A BK Currents Book

This book is part of our BK Currents series. BK Currents books advance social and economic justice by exploring the critical intersections between business and society. Offering a unique combination of thoughtful analysis and progressive alternatives, BK Currents books promote positive change at the national and global levels. To find out more, visit **www.bkconnection.com**.

Berrett–Koehler
Publishers

Connecting people and ideas
to create a world that works for all

Dear Reader,

Thank you for picking up this book and joining our worldwide community of Berrett-Koehler readers. We share ideas that bring positive change into people's lives, organizations, and society.

To welcome you, we'd like to offer you a free e-book. You can pick from among twelve of our bestselling books by entering the promotional code **BKP92E** here: http://www.bkconnection.com/welcome.

When you claim your free e-book, we'll also send you a copy of our e-newsletter, the *BK Communiqué*. Although you're free to unsubscribe, there are many benefits to sticking around. In every issue of our newsletter you'll find

- A free e-book
- Tips from famous authors
- Discounts on spotlight titles
- Hilarious insider publishing news
- A chance to win a prize for answering a riddle

Best of all, our readers tell us, "Your newsletter is the only one I actually read." So claim your gift today, and please stay in touch!

Sincerely,

Charlotte Ashlock
Steward of the BK Website

Questions? Comments? Contact me at bkcommunity@bkpub.com.